Mrs. Kelly's
JOURNEY HOME

Stories of an American family

Mrs. Kelly's
JOURNEY HOME

Stories of an American family

By
Breeda Kelly Miller

© 2024 by Breeda Kelly Miller

Published by Soar 2 Success Publishing

Soar2SuccessPublishing.com

All rights reserved. Except as permitted under the US Copyright Act of 1976, no part of this publication may be reproduced, distributed, or transmitted in any form or by any means, or stored in a database or retrieval system, without the prior written permission of the author.

ISBN: 978-1-956465-23-5

Printed in the United States of America

Front cover credits: Thomas J. Kelly & Scott Wasserman
Back cover credits: Darcel Swekel Demyanovich

CONTENTS

Introduction ix

Part 1. The Journey Begins 1

Part 2. A New Journey 121

Part 3. A Caregiver's Journey 173

Acknowledgments 191

INTRODUCTION

I don't think I could ever write a novel. I don't have the imagination for fiction and that's why you can rest assured that all the stories in this book are true. The people are real and the things they said and did actually happened. I just couldn't make them up. Now, I did take some time frames and squish them together to keep the stories moving along, but the truth is often stranger, and funnier, than fiction.

That said, I hope you enjoy this journey half as much as I have. I hope that you find yourself, your family, and your journey in this book and that it might inspire you to record those precious stories either on video, in a notebook, or just written on the back of old photos. I believe that honoring our past helps us build our future. Plus, my mom wrote down several of these stories and then wrote a note at the end: "For your future book! Love, Mom." That was in 2007.

This book is a promise I made to myself as I created the play *Mrs. Kelly's Journey Home*. As I wrote and revised, each edit removed stories or details that just wouldn't fit into a 90-minute play. I felt guilty and comforted myself by promising to include those details and extra stories in the book I would eventually write. My hope is that this book of very personal journeys will resonate with you. I do believe that we all have great stories in our lives. We just need to take the time to consider our experiences, remember them, and learn from them. I do think that ordinary experiences can make for extraordinary stories.

Breeda Miller

Breeda Kelly Miller
December 2024

DEDICATION

This book is dedicated to my family in Ireland and in America.

My parents, my brothers, my children, and my beloved Jim, without whom none of this would have been possible.

For all the immigrants who struggle to fit in and for all the caregivers who struggle to survive, may your strength and courage be remembered as acts of faith and love.

Part 1
THE JOURNEY BEGINS

Tom and Mary Kelly at the sea in Rush,
County Dublin, Ireland, 1989

Mrs. Kelly's Journey Home

Two brave souls emigrated from Ireland to America in order to provide a better life for their children. They knew no one. They didn't have family to guide them. They had faith in God and in each other and in the American Dream. The courage to leave one's native home, family, and friends to explore a land across an ocean boggles the minds of most people. Life in Ireland in the 1950s was a struggle. Jobs were scarce and unlike the rest of Europe, Ireland didn't benefit from The Marshall Plan to rebuild Europe following World War II due to their neutrality. Tom and Mary Kelly's decision in 1956 to pack up and move to America set in motion a series of events that impacted lives on four continents. Marriages, births, and adoptions were all made possible by a singular decision of these two immigrants. This is their story.

<< Mary Kelly, age 7, in her first communion outfit, handmade by her Auntie Lilly, 1932

Mary Philomena Byrne was born to Rosemary and Henry Byrne on April 12, 1925, Easter Sunday in Dublin, Ireland. Because she was born on Easter, many said she should be called Ester, but her mother would have none of that. Her first-born daughter would be called Mary, as was the custom in most Irish Catholic families at the time. The Byrne clan grew to consist of three boys and three girls, and they lived in a number of homes around the North side of Dublin. The final family home was in Prospect Square in Glasnevin, adjacent to Glasnevin Cemetery. A brick row house, it sat across the cobblestone square from one of Dublin's oldest pubs, Kavanagh's, known as The Gravediggers Pub. The Pub had a small window on the wall backing up to the cemetery. After a long night of digging, pints would be passed through the window to the thirsty workers as they were too dirty to come inside. This historic cemetery was the neighborhood playground, and the Byrne kids played all day amongst the headstones and monuments.

When little Mary Philomena was born, she was so tiny the doctors weren't sure she would live. She was indeed a survivor, a title she wore proudly. Her petite stature was always a point of pride, much to my embarrassment as my shape favored the Kelly side. I always felt huge next to my mother. At doctor visits later in life, I winced as she made sure to inform the doctor that she was special and that she couldn't take regular doses of medicine because she had miniature organs. One of her favorite sayings was, "Good goods come in small parcels."

Rosemary Byrne died of a stroke when Mary was just 21. As the eldest, she was expected to raise her brothers and sisters. So, she did. Her father worked, and the Byrne children were educated by the Christian Brothers and the Holy Faith sisters. The Byrne kids didn't know they were poor by today's standards. They didn't have any toys. They played with paper dolls for hours and spent evenings listening to the "wireless." Mary's father took her into Dublin one day to see the exhibition of Marconi's first radio.

Life in Dublin was busy. They were able to take the double-decker buses into the city center to go shopping in the massive department store on O'Connell Street, Clery's. The traditional spot to meet up with friends was under the clock at Clery's. They walked everywhere and enjoyed going to the picture show in town. The seaside was just a few stops away on the bus route.

While Mary and her two sisters attended the Holy Faith Convent school, which had a stellar reputation for academics, she told me that when she and her sisters were walking in Dublin, they kept their heads down and walked quickly past the tall stone walls of the convent of the Magdalene Sisters. It was home to the infamous Magdalene Laundry. They didn't know what happened on the other side of the wall; they just knew it wasn't good. The Magdalene Laundries were essentially workhouses throughout Ireland that used the labor of young women to run the service. Decades later, the abuse of young girls, many of whom were pregnant, was revealed. The treatment of the young women and the babies they bore, who were taken from them, was a national disgrace.

Mary met Tom Kelly when she worked in the office of a Dublin print shop and he was a printer. She was just twenty-two. In high contrast to the affable Byrne family, the Kellys lived in a different world, though it was only a few miles up the road. The Kellys were from Wexford and had moved to Dublin when Tom Kelly was a teenager. The family consisted of nine children, including one set of twin girls. Tom attended the Christian Brother's school and was treated harshly, along with all the other boys. He was an intelligent boy who loved to read. The Kellys were well known throughout Dublin for their intellect and quirky personalities. Following in his father's and brother's footsteps, Tom became a printer. He worked in small print shops as an apprentice for many years before landing a job with the Irish Independent, a Dublin newspaper. He loved it, but he wanted more.

The Kelly siblings in Dublin, 1945

When Tom introduced Mary, the petite Dubliner, to his family, their response was less than enthusiastic. "So, you're the Dub," was all his father had to say. They were hoping Tom would find a big, strapping girl from the country who was also a nurse.

Their courtship was spent attending local dances and riding around Dublin on Tom's motorcycle. Tom gave Mary two fabulous engagement gifts—a sparkling black bicycle (no chrome due to the war) and an English Springer Spaniel puppy. He knew her well.

Mrs. Kelly's JOURNEY HOME

Newly-engaged Mary Byrne
with her new bike

Mrs. Kelly's JOURNEY HOME

Mary with her beloved Corrib, 1947

They were married in 1947 in the Iona Road Church. There were so many Catholic Churches in Dublin that they were almost never called by their proper name; instead, they were known by the name of the road they were on. My parents had a typical Irish wedding in the late forties. It was a morning Mass followed by a nice luncheon. Due to the war, brides didn't wear fancy white gowns, but they dressed up and celebrated just the same. A honeymoon in Galway followed, and the happy couple moved in with Mary's father and siblings in Glasnevin, the heart of Dublin.

Tom and Mary's wedding, 1947

Mrs. Kelly's JOURNEY HOME

Mary's favorite place—the Irish seaside. Donagh was off to explore, Brendan needed a cuddle, and David was having a hard time. She loved it all.

The young Kelly family lived in the charming brick-row houses in Glasnevin with Mary's father, Henry Byrne. No central heating but each room had a small fireplace. Soon they had a young family, three rambunctious boys. David, Donagh, and Brendan. Mary's best friend, Florence (Flor), lived a few doors down and she had three kids as well. Mary loved babies and children and enjoyed playing with them. They spent so many wonderful days at the seaside. Flor didn't have the patience for young children and preferred to spend her time cleaning the house. So, they traded. Mary took Flor's three along with her own and spent the day at the park while Flor cleaned both their houses. Mary's floors were sparkling, and Flor's kids were exhausted and ready for a bath and bed. It was a brilliant plan.

Tom had a good job at the newspaper, and they were able to purchase their first home in Kilbarrack on the north side of Dublin, near Howth. They were just steps from the Irish Sea, accessible through the legendary "hole in the wall." The boys were in school, and Mary loved taking care of their home. She finally had her own garden. The brick bungalow had both a front and back garden with a large bay window. They were the first in the neighborhood to purchase a television set, and the boys' favorite programs were the American westerns, *Gunsmoke* and all the rest. Life was good.

Mrs. Kelly's JOURNEY HOME

Their first TV in Ireland

My parents had a traditional Irish marriage. That meant that my father made the decisions, and my mother was expected to go along. The day he arrived home from work at the Dublin newspaper and announced they were moving to America was a perfect example. Tom had dreamt of following the American Dream. It was the 1950s and jobs were scarce in Ireland. He had a good job as a master printer, but he wanted a more secure future for his sons. It wasn't up for discussion.

The Irish exodus wasn't limited to the Great Famine in the 1850s. While the situation wasn't as dire, in the 1950s, economic opportunities weren't great, and many families felt compelled to leave their homeland to seek their fortunes elsewhere. Ireland's greatest export has been its people. Nearly 80 million people worldwide claim Irish ancestry. More than 36 million Americans claim Irish as their primary ethnicity. One hundred years after the Great Famine, the Kelly family joined this statistical group.

The day Tom arrived home from work and made the big announcement, it took Mary's breath away. Tom told her that an agent from Canada was recruiting for the Toronto Star newspaper, and they would pay high wages and ship's passage for skilled master printers to emigrate. The thing was, he would have to enter Canada under a British quota. That didn't sit well with him. He was a fiercely proud Irishman, and this was an affront to his nationality. However, he realized this was his big chance and he didn't want to miss it. Mary was speechless. She couldn't imagine leaving her home, her brothers and sisters, her beloved dog, and her father, who wasn't well. But in those days, the wife was simply expected to follow her husband. It broke her heart.

She knew times were tough. Many of her friends and family were emigrating. Her brother, Gerard, had just left for New Zealand in search of work. Tom left for Canada soon after, and Mary's father moved in with her and the boys. So many changes. She didn't like them. She didn't choose them.

My parents and brothers emigrated from Ireland in the late 1950s. Tom Kelly was a master printer who used bars of hot lead type to lay out a full-size newspaper and then proofread it, backward. My mother, Mary Kelly, was a charming, articulate woman, just five feet tall, with an extraordinarily positive outlook, despite being married to a pretty contrary man who could find the worst in just about any situation. In America, they were oil and water. In Ireland, they were chalk and cheese. I often called my parents' marriage an endurance contest rather than a union, but I am getting ahead of myself.

Mrs. Kelly's JOURNEY HOME

Thomas J. Kelly, printer, 1956

Thomas J. Kelly grew up in a very large, very strict family with nine children. His mother had to manage the household and she (according to my mother) had locks on all the kitchen cabinets to keep the food stores safe from snacking children. He became a printer the same as his father and most of his brothers. It was said the Kellys had ink rather than blood in their veins. It was a noble profession and took great skill to use the lead type in the Linotype machines to lay out the newspapers and printed materials. He had aspirations for his family and believed that America was the place to fulfill his dreams. After he arrived in Canada, he aggressively sought opportunities in the States. He wrote to anyone he knew and inquired about printing jobs. A friend in Detroit wrote back about a job in the composing room of the Detroit Free Press. He knew nothing of Detroit other than it was called the Motor City. He found his way there and decided that Michigan was the place to be. That was how our family ended up living here, a random letter from an acquaintance.

As Mary and Tom emigrated to America, her brother Gerard left for New Zealand. Well, he meant to go to New Zealand, but the ship stopped in South Africa and he decided that was far enough and he would stay there. He sent for his Dublin girlfriend; they married and had two sons. They lived in Cape Town for the rest of their lives.

Mary's youngest sister, Bridget, who was always called Betty, came to Detroit on a visit and met a handsome Italian American. They married and the family in Ireland had a very hard time pronouncing her new name, Betty Biancucci. Her brother Ronnie emigrated to Canada, but he and his wife didn't stay long. They returned to Dublin after only a few years on this side of the ocean. They missed the charm and "craic" of home too much. Only one other member of the Kellys emigrated: his younger brother Paddy. Paddy and his family lived in Philadelphia for a few years, but when the opportunity arose to return to Ireland and manage an estate for an American, they moved back "home."

Mrs. Kelly's JOURNEY HOME

Tom and his mother, Anastasia Kelly, 1969

Tom's widowed mother, Anastasia, lived alone for many years in a two-story house in Marino, near Fairview Park, in Dublin. Every September,

Tom would send her money to purchase coal for her fireplaces as the house did not have central heating. His brothers never forgave him for leaving Ireland, believing he thought it wasn't good enough for him, but he was always a fiercely proud Irishman. Granny Kelly was a serious woman who admired her highly intelligent, if quirky, offspring. Her eldest son, Christy, known as the "mad genius," was widely respected for his intellect and a bit feared for his personality. He was a printer like his father and most of his brothers. There were nine Kellys born to Anastasia and Clement, three girls and six boys. It was a hard life. My mother always said that Granny Kelly never liked children. Could be why.

"Holy Christ Tonight!" Tom exclaimed when he spoke of his experience in Canada. He just wanted to get to America, and Canada was a total shock to his system. Here he was on the other side of the Atlantic, surrounded by the Brits! Pictures of the queen everywhere, Union Jacks on display, and he even saw signs that said, "No Irish Need Apply." He couldn't wait to get to America. He had a buddy in Detroit, Michigan, who wrote to him about a job at the Detroit Free Press. Tom took a train to Windsor and then a bus across the bridge over the Detroit River to see about the job. The minute he set foot in the Motor City, he loved it. It was so different from home. Big cars everywhere, music like he'd never heard, and food he never knew existed. He transferred to the newspaper in Windsor and lived there while he applied for his visa to work in America. It took a long time, over a year, but he would take the bus to Detroit and he discovered a very special place, The Gaelic League. It was as if he'd come home. Surrounded by fellow Irish immigrants, he settled in. The pints of lager didn't hurt his adjustment either.

Tom riding in a friend's convertible in the Motor City, 1957

Meanwhile, across the ocean, Mary was managing the household, caring for her father, her beloved dog, and three young boys. On her own. She was exhausted. Now she had to pack up their home, sell the house, leave her father and her dog, and join Tom in Detroit. I can't imagine how she was able to do it all. She was leaving her family and the only place she'd ever lived. She was getting on an airplane for the first time to fly over the ocean to a country where she knew no one. She told me, with tears in her eyes, "The day I left Ireland was the saddest day in my life. Right up there with the day my mother died." The flights to America left from Shannon Airport in the center of Ireland. They lived in Dublin on the East Coast. Her family and friends had to book taxis to take them to the airport to say goodbye. A caravan of taxis filled with family and friends. Everybody was crying. They had no idea when they would see her again. She had no idea what lay ahead of her.

The flight to America was a nightmare. Twelve hours in PanAm's best—a propeller plane. It was not a smooth flight. She was on her own with three young boys climbing over and under the seats, upset tummies, and plenty of tears. She was a wreck when they finally landed in Detroit. Tom was there to greet them at the gate. He herded them into a big taxi because he had no car. As they headed down the highway to their new rental home, the boys couldn't contain themselves. They pressed their noses against the windows and kept asking, "Where are the cowboys? Where are the cowboys?" The only cowboy ever sighted on I-94 was the massive Marlboro Man billboard, and that was years later.

In Ireland, the boys were getting ready for America with a friend.

Tom had rented a small home near the bus line just south of Detroit. He'd purchased a few beds and some secondhand furniture. He didn't think to get a lamp and there were no overhead lights. They spent their first night in America in the dark. Mary cried herself to sleep that night. What could she do? She couldn't go home; she'd sold everything. The next morning was Sunday, and as a devout Catholic, she needed to get her family to Mass. Their new neighbors, the Loritzes, were kind people who loaned them a spare lamp from their basement and offered to drive them to church. The tricky bit was that the Loritzes weren't Catholic and had no idea where the nearest Catholic Church was. Unlike Ireland, there was a huge variety of churches in America. The Loritzes drove the Kellys around the city to about ten different churches before landing on a Catholic one. This church tour hit Mary hard. She wasn't in Ireland any longer.

Mrs. Kelly's JOURNEY HOME

> Tom Kelly loved America the moment he set foot across the border. He found a small Italian restaurant near their new home that had a bar upholstered in dark red vinyl. He discovered pizza, something he'd never seen much less tasted, and he loved it. He couldn't wait to share this "real *American* treat" with his boys. They had been in the States about a week when he brought home a large, deluxe Clemente's pizza. It was loaded. The boys stood 'round as he opened the big, flat box and the steam escaped. Then Brendan, the youngest, burst into tears. "It looks like somebody threw up on bread!" he cried. My father ate that first pizza by himself. They wouldn't touch it. Soon enough, they were brave and tried lots of new things. Pizza became their favorite.

The adjustment to life in America was huge. Mary had enrolled her boys in a Catholic school (with the help of the Loritzes), but she missed one important detail. My brothers had attended an all-boys Catholic school in Ireland. Things were different in America, and David's first day didn't go so well. He arrived home in floods of tears and was so upset he couldn't even tell her what had happened. She finally got it out of him that he was upset because he had to sit next to a girl in class all day. He had never been in a class with girls. This same situation didn't bother my brother Donagh a bit. My mom reassured David that she would call the Reverend Mother and get it sorted. She called the school office and explained the situation to Sister Modesta and asked if David's seat could be moved next to a boy until he adjusted to the "situation." The Reverend Mother agreed, and David drank his tea as he wiped his eyes.

My parents always referred to Ireland as "home." I never heard them calling Ireland the "old country" as so many other immigrants referred to their homeland. I've never understood this difference, but I found it striking. Whether it was due to a different language or pronunciation, I don't know, but I felt it and noticed it. The word "home" was almost a prayer.

My brothers just wanted to fit in. Sports were a huge challenge. They didn't know anything about baseball or basketball, and the football they knew was called soccer here and nobody was playing it in 1957. In time, they lost their accents. Donagh became Don. They learned new sports and made friends in the neighborhood. America was becoming home.

The Kelly boys make new friends in the neighborhood.

As immigrants, my parents had huge advantages. They were white, they spoke English, and most Americans found their accents charming. Still, cultural differences and the lack of family support made daily life challenging.

Tom took the bus each morning to his job in Detroit. While the boys were in school, Mary was home alone in a strange country in a new house. She had no family here and knew no one. Eventually, they found a little house to purchase just south of Detroit. They bought it on a land contract, trusting that the deal was sound. It was not. As immigrants, they were taken advantage of and spent years making house payments that never went to actually paying off the house. Many years later, after receiving letters of eviction for non-payment, Mary took charge and found an attorney (an Irish-American friend from the Gaelic League) who helped them and saved their home. Starting a new life in a new country without any guidance was a rough journey indeed.

Language mattered in my family. My parents didn't have much formal education, but they were avid readers, and pronunciation and diction were very important in the Kelly home.

However, my parents never failed to swap out the t's and the th's. "Thanks" was just "Tanks." "Three and third" was "tree and a turd." But God forbid I say a midwestern "steers" for stairs or "liberry." I was corrected every time. In later years, my mom always called the little antacid tablets, "Thumbs." I never corrected her.

I was devastated to learn that "amn't" wasn't a proper word in America. At school, Sister called me up to the front of the room and told me that I couldn't use that word as it wasn't a real word. Mortified, I tried to make my case. Surely a contraction of "am" and "not" should be "amn't." Ever so much nicer than "ain't," which my friends said all the time. She wasn't buying it. I was six.

But I think the insults were the best. Mary's opinions of others were…colorful. Which was fine, except when she forgot and used her "Outside Voice." We saw a woman with a very big hairstyle—you know, teased and sticking up. Mary's comment: "She looks as if the rats were sucking on her hair all night!" Another poor soul: "She's no oil painting." An older woman in younger women's clothes: "Mutton dressed as lamb."

Tom loved words as well and he even made up his own. Crabby old women were called "bedulas." Annoying young children were "banticles." His favorite expression was "Holy Christ Tonight!" I never understood what it meant. He referred to most people as "eejits" and "little gets," and his favorite toast was the traditional Irish "Slainte," which means good health.

Decades later, a common Irish expression of agreement, "I know it well," caused a bit of confusion for a neighbor. The popular Irish author, Maeve Binchy, was becoming known in America. A neighbor asked Mary whether she had heard of her. Mary's quick response was, "Ah yes! I know her well." That neighbor was excited to tell me that my mother knew Maeve Binchy personally and probably grew up with her. Not so much. Just missing the little word "of" made a big difference. Even speaking the same language caused a "lost in translation" moment.

When my brothers received their first American report cards from Christ the Good Shepherd Catholic School, they were in deep trouble. The elementary school report card had a list of behaviors and skills with boxes that were checked by the teacher. My brothers brought home their cards filled with "tick marks" and were immediately banished to their rooms and punished. In Ireland, a "tick mark" or a check mark was a bad thing and meant this was unfinished or substandard. However, in America, those same "tick marks" meant the opposite. My brothers had been well educated in Ireland and they were at grade level or above their classmates. My parents didn't understand this grading system and thought their boys were acting up and not doing their work. Whether it was through a parent/teacher conference or a phone call with the Reverend Mother, they learned their sons were indeed bright boys and were acclimating nicely with good grades. I doubt that my father apologized to them, and I noticed they preferred to stand rather than sit for several days.

Lost in Translation?

Between slang and familiar expressions, communication was often a challenge. Some things didn't translate at all.

Irish	American
Biscuits	Cookies
Togs	Swimsuit
Trainers	Tennis shoes
Runners	Sneakers
Porridge	Oatmeal
Loo	Bathroom
Chips	French fries
Crisps	Chips
Car boot	Car trunk
Craic	Good fun
Bunburger	Hamburger
Unwell	Sick
Homely	Cozy
Rashers	Bacon
Bacon	Ham
Jumper	Sweater
Getting the messages	Running errands

**Mary with her hands full,
four kids and a dog.**

Shortly after moving into their new little brick home, I was born. It was cause for celebration, much to the annoyance of my brothers, I'm sure. After ten boys on both sides of the family, I was the first granddaughter born all the way in America. Mary often said I was her "Gift from Uncle Sam." I was the apple of my father's eye and he called me "Beeswing." I was named after Mary's sister, Bridget, who was always called Betty. Breeda is the Irish version of Bridget. It's usually spelled Breda, but my mom was concerned that I would be called "Breada," so she added another "e." That's why my name is spelled Breeda. It never occurred to her that when Americans read my name, they usually think it's Brenda, misspelled.

Breeda's first birthday, 1959

I'd call my mom a homemaker rather than a housewife. She wasn't a fancy cook, but we were always well-fed—especially when it came to her baking. She could make scones and soda bread with her eyes closed. Her brown bread was legendary. But it was her pie—her apple pie—that was her crowning achievement. She truly had magic fingers, and she used to turn out a delicate flaky pastry with a scoop of flour and a lump of butter. She cooked porridge every morning, so when I read the *Harry Potter* books to my kids, I didn't have to explain what porridge was, as well as many other terms that Americans might not have immediately understood.

But one dish that my father adored and my mother cooked for him drove me out of the house the minute she put the big pot on the stove. Tripe. Boiled tripe. The stench of boiled cow stomach and the look of a large plate of it covered in white sauce was the most nauseating thing I had ever seen or smelled. Worse than liver and onions, which he devoured as well. Dinner was always pretty straightforward: meat, potatoes, and a vegetable—all served steaming hot. If she wanted to make an American casserole dish, usually with elbow macaroni, she also had to prepare a separate meal (meat, potatoes, and a veg) for my dad. Potatoes were often served with their "jackets" on, and my father insisted on a separate plate for the potato peels. We had a very small kitchen, and the table groaned under the weight of all the different plates. But she made it all happen. We were never hungry.

She loved to garden and filled our little house with plants. My father hated those plants. He didn't mind them outside, but bringing them inside was more than he could handle.

Mrs. Kelly's Journey Home

The Scourge of Houseplants

Tom Kelly: "This house is like a bloody jungle. I can't even find a place to set down a cup of tea with all the pots and leaves everywhere. They're sucking all the oxygen out of the room! Mary loves them, she even talks to them, all lovey-dovey and sweet. Christ Tonight! Says it makes them grow bigger. Hmmph. I have me own plan. When she's out, I talk to them as well. I curse at them and tell them to stay in their pots and out of my way. I don't mind the garden outside and I enjoy watering the plants. In fact, when one of our boys took a trip out west and was gone for a few months, he asked me to water the plants in his back garden. He had a miserable space hidden behind his garage with a few plants. Sorriest excuse for tomato plants I ever saw. Not a single tomato all summer and I went over and watered them regularly."

My mother got a good chuckle from this situation. She knew those were no more tomato plants than she was the Queen of England. He was watering a few illegal plants—weeds, if you know what I'm saying. I don't think they ever told him what they were.

A knock on the side door opened up her world. Her new neighbor, an outgoing redhead named Virginia Wilson, came to welcome her. Mrs. Wilson was pregnant with her sixth child and had already met my brothers because they were running around the neighborhood with her boys. My mother called the Wilsons "the salt of the earth." Mary Kelly didn't know how to drive, didn't really know anything about America. She didn't even drink coffee, but the Wilsons loved to listen to her accent and welcomed her (and all of us) with open arms.

Raymond and Virginia Wilson

The Wilsons took the Kelly family under their wing. Virginia was a homemaker and her husband, Raymond, was a long-haul truck driver. They attended the same Catholic church. The Kellys learned a lot about being American from the Wilsons. The big family shared their lives, inviting the immigrants for their big taco night festivities. An assembly line of sizzling ground beef, shredded cheese, chopped lettuce, tomatoes, onions, and crispy corn shells was a new experience and a huge treat for the Irish family who had never even heard of a taco. Small details like never drinking coffee (only tea with milk) and big challenges like not knowing how to drive a car were made easier by these kind and generous neighbors. Unlike Ireland, America was huge and everything was so far away. The stores were enormous and filled with unfamiliar foods and packages. Nothing was easy.

Mrs. Wilson gave birth to her sixth child shortly after the Kellys moved in. She was a beautiful baby girl and they named her Mary Christina. She was born with Down's syndrome. Virginia Wilson was in shock. She knew about babies, but this baby was so sick and so tiny she didn't know what to do. The baby was blind, diabetic, and had heart problems. Her Down's syndrome was severe, and she never said a single word, not even "mama." Mary Kelly showed up on her doorstep the day after she arrived home from the hospital. She scooped Mary Christina into her arms and soothed her. It was Mary Kelly who gave this sweet baby her first bath. From that moment, Mary and Virginia became a dynamic duo. Tom wasn't home much, and Mrs. Wilson was her ticket to freedom. Virginia drove and Mary rode. Mary often said she never had any idea where they were going. They would pile kids into the back of the Wilsons' station wagon and head off for garage sales and visits to the Detroit Riverfront. A magical mystery tour!

As Mary would say, "Virginia Wilson was the genuine article!" A lifelong Detroiter, she grew up in a section of Detroit called Corktown—which Mary thought was just amazing. Early Irish immigrants from Cork settled in this section of Detroit, hence the nickname. The Wilsons loved to camp. They even invited Mary to go with them. She'd never been camping before but was getting more independent. She just told Tom she was going with them, and she went. She made sure she packed her tea bags, and she was ready to go. They took her to the Upper Peninsula of Michigan. She had never seen so many trees in her life. She would stay in the camper with Mary Christina while they went off fishing or hiking. She said she would never forget the first time they took her to the dump to feed the bears. "An actual dump with real live bears!" she exclaimed. She was terrified.

On one of their outings, Mary and Virginia discovered the Penrickton School for the Blind for Mary Christina. I went with them when they volunteered at the school. I will never forget the first time I needed to use the toilet at the school. Now, a school for blind children didn't need privacy in the bathroom. There was just a row of tiny toilets with no stalls. I was four and I was embarrassed to use the toilet in front of all the other children. Until my mother reminded me that they were all blind and couldn't see me.

Virginia and Mary were a dynamic duo, and they volunteered at the Eloise Psychiatric Hospital, known as the Eloise Asylum, in Westland, Michigan. There were various holiday parties for the patients, but the Halloween Party was the highlight of the year for them and for the residents. Both women dressed in costumes, and I remember a particularly scary Raggedy Ann and Andy getup. The Hobo costumes one year were quite authentic-looking, burned cork providing the appropriate unshaven look. My job was to help prepare the party favors. The favorite one was truly a sign of the times, the 1960s: two cigarettes wrapped in tin foil with a little bow tying it closed. It was quite festive and very popular with the patients. I spent days opening packs of cigarettes and wrapping up the little packages. They filled two large baskets along with chocolates and other treats. The cigarettes went first.

They joined the Christian Mothers group at church and spent a lot of time working the rummage sales. Mary loved it because they got first dibs on everything. With four growing children, she needed to spend money wisely. They went through the sixties together learning TM, Transcendental Meditation—Mary was very proud of having her own mantra. They even smoked marijuana once in Virginia's basement, "just to see what the fuss [was] all about." They joined NOW (National Organization of Women) and got political. Petitions, marches, campaigns—the Equal Rights Amendment. Mary took a few classes at the local community college with Virginia. They even went to see the musical *Hair* in downtown Detroit. They did it all, whether their husbands liked it or not.

On one of their less fortunate adventures, Mary unwittingly became a blonde. Virginia's cousin, Rita, was studying to be a hairdresser and needed some practice. So, on one of their little outings, Rita asked if Mary would help her out and have her do her hair. Mary had no idea that the bleach and then blonde dye would not wash out and was mortified to learn that her beautiful, shiny black hair was permanently blonde—at least until it grew a bit and she needed a touch-up. Over a decade of purple bleach paste in our kitchen applied by me (!) kept her in that look. A look she really hated, but she thought there was no going back. I'm not sure how she learned that she could go back to her natural color, but she was thrilled to be rid of the monthly ritual of bleaching and dying her hair. I still have an aversion to the smell of that purple paste.

**Breeda, J.F., and blonde Mary
at the Detroit Zoo, 1971**

Many years later, Mary's sister Lillie came for a visit from Dublin. Virginia organized a night out at what Mary thought was a fancy restaurant. Chippendales. She hadn't a clue. While the other women enjoyed the male dancers and gleefully stuffed dollar bills in their G strings, Mary was mortified. Then they got her up on stage with the male dancers. She made the sign of the cross and closed her eyes. I don't think she ever told my father about this night out.

Mrs. Kelly's JOURNEY HOME

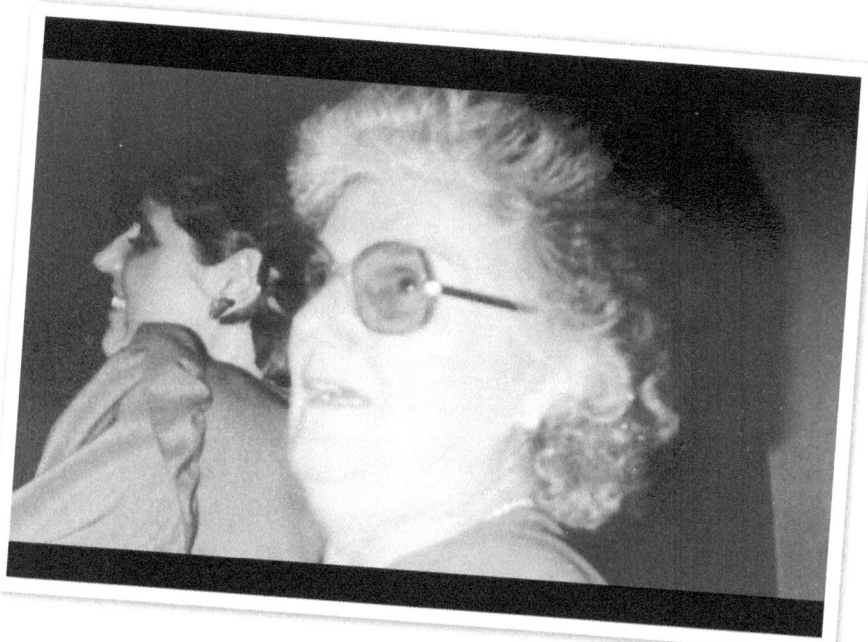

Whaaaaat?

She was mortified.

Our home was filled with the antics of five children, and when things inevitably broke, no one wanted to own up to it. My father would become frustrated and say sarcastically, "I suppose Mrs. Wilson broke it!" We would all nod silently. Poor Mrs. Wilson did a lot of damage over the years.

In 1968, my parents became U.S. citizens, and my mother asked Virginia to be her sponsor. Mary Kelly carried her voter's registration card with her always and never missed an election. She never learned to drive but she certainly learned to vote; she took her role as a U.S. citizen very seriously. When my eldest brother left to serve our country in Vietnam, my mother said she had never felt such pride. He returned home safely, and many years later, my youngest brother, John, enlisted as well. As my mother often said, "We love America, warts and all!" She had come a long way in a short time.

Mrs. Kelly's JOURNEY HOME

David T. Kelly, U.S. Air Force, heading off to Vietnam, 1969

Mrs. Kelly's JOURNEY HOME

John Fitzgerald Kelly, U.S. Air Force, 1986

Mrs. Kelly's JOURNEY HOME

Mary Kelly never learned to drive, though she tried. She really did. Her Irish friend, Ellen Cullen, wanted to learn and convinced her to take a driving course. It did not end well. It was an absolute miracle that no one died during their practice sessions. Stories of ending up in ditches and my brothers taking her out to drive in the neighborhood were family lore, as my father refused to do so. One day, my brother Donagh, always a joker, as well as a skilled mechanic, decided to have a bit of fun. He took Mom out for a practice drive heading to the high school parking lot. As they entered the empty parking lot (he was driving), she told him he was driving too fast. He told her, "Okay, then *you* drive." He popped off the steering wheel (which he had loosened in advance) and handed the steering wheel to Mary, who was terrified in the passenger seat. She never got over the shock and he thought it was the best story ever.

Mrs. Kelly's JOURNEY HOME

Before the dreaded driveway incident

She was near the end of her course and needed more driving experience. Tom had refused to take her out to drive, but one Sunday morning, he relented. We were driving home from Mass on a lovely, sunny spring morning. No traffic, a straight road home. I was in the backseat. No turns or tricky maneuvers. We reached our home with Tom sitting in the passenger seat bracing both hands on the dashboard the entire time. She clicked the turn signal to turn into the narrow driveway. My brother's friend was visiting and her small sports car (a Karmann Ghia) was parked on the tiny spot next to the actual driveway. Tom began barking at Mary to watch out for Chris's car and then it happened. She stepped on the gas pedal rather than the brake, turned the steering wheel right into the corner of the Fergusons' house. No one was injured, the house sustained a minor dent, and she never got behind the wheel again.

Mary Kelly Quotes

Your ship will come in!
I see the glass half full.
Biff, Bang, Biff!
I could murder a cup of tea!
I'll box your ears for you.
Don't be a sheep.
What's the Catch-22?
Jesus, Mary, and Joseph!
Merciful Hour.
She looks as though the rats were sucking on her hair.
I could do without this.
I have miniature organs.
I don't want to be mutton dressed as lamb.

Immigrants celebrating holidays, many of them for the very first time, presents a unique challenge. Thanksgiving was an entirely foreign experience. The idea of putting pumpkin in a pie was absolutely appalling to my mother; even the addition of cinnamon to an apple pie was unheard of in Ireland. With five hungry mouths to feed and a husband who had high expectations for a feast, the pressure was on. My mom knew how to roast a turkey. Mashed potatoes and gravy were no problem. It was the side dishes and the desserts that were migraine-inducing. Stuffing in America is called dressing in Ireland, and cranberry sauce was a complete mystery. However, my mother was up for the challenge, and she managed to pull off the feast and we and the big bird were stuffed. This was the end of November and she was already exhausted with several family birthdays on the calendar as well.

Mary Kelly feeding us all from her tiny kitchen

Mary's biggest complaint was that in less than a month, she had to do it all over again. The expectation of a big Christmas dinner, with a menu that was almost identical to Thanksgiving, save for the required ham that my father insisted on as well as the big turkey, nearly put her over the edge.

When my friends would talk about their Christmas tradition of loading up in their car to make the rounds of grandparents, aunts, uncles, and cousins, I had no idea what they were talking about. All I could think of was how hard it must have been for them to leave their home (and new toys) on Christmas Day to visit all their relatives. For my family, it was just us. We had no aunts, uncles, cousins, or grandparents to visit. My mom had no one to bring side dishes or help with the "heavy cooking" until I got older. My father and my brothers were great at consuming the meal but not so great at helping with the prep and clean-up. It was a perspective that never struck me as unusual as it was just the way it was. We did leave the house to go to Mass on Christmas morning, until I was old enough to attend Midnight Mass on Christmas Eve. That was a huge rite of passage, and I remember how grown up I felt coming out of the church in the middle of the night with the snow falling. We didn't have to rush to go places and share this day.

As we grew older and my brothers married and I dated Jim, we had to share our solitary holiday and experience other families' traditions. Mostly, it went well, and we adapted our traditions and added new ones. When Jim and I first began dating, I learned that his family celebrated the holiday on Christmas Eve, and because my family didn't do anything special on Christmas Eve, it was a smooth adaptation. It was Miller time on Christmas Eve and we were with the Kellys on Christmas Day. If only all family challenges could be resolved so smoothly.

Mary Kelly was a woman of great faith in God and in herself. She always said she was blessed and that her faith sustained her. Her favorite prayer was simply "Jesus, Mary, and Joseph." She said it all the time. Some Americans thought this was taking the Lord's name in vain. It's actually a short prayer for divine intervention. She'd make a quick sign of the cross for additional support when needed, and if it was really serious, it was "Jesus, Mary, and HOLY St. Joseph." Watch out. She always carried a rosary, and whenever we faced a challenge, she would tell us, "I'll say a rosary for you." I would often call her and request a special "lap of the beads." One time it was very important, and I told her I expected to see callouses on her fingers.

I was so proud of my uniform and leather school bag going off on the bus each morning to Christ the Good Shephard Catholic School. Every morning before I could leave the house, I had to recite my Guardian Angel prayer, even if it meant keeping the bus waiting.

Breeda Kelly heading off to first grade, 1963

> *Angel of God, my guardian dear*
> *To whom God's love commits me here*
> *Ever this day be at my side*
> *To light, to rule, to guard and guide*

I never remember my brothers having to say it. But in later years, I made my kids say it, too. Mom always said goodbye with a simple, breathy, "God Bless!" which was short for "May God bless us and save us all."

On those rare occasions when my father went to Mass with us, he was always a bit too quick and too loud when the priest finally announced, "The Mass is ended. Go in peace."

"TANKS BE TO GOD!" he'd say. We had to sit in the back so he could make a quick exit for a smoke.

Tea in Ireland is not just a nice warm beverage; it's nearly a sacrament. My mother believed a nice cup of tea was the solution to almost every problem. "Are you cold? Tea will warm you. Are you tired? Tea will wake you. Can't sleep? Tea will help. If you are celebrating, or just wanting to relax, tea is the answer."

Ordering tea in American restaurants was what made my mother a coffee drinker. She called the warmed water in a tiny metal pot with an anemic tea bag, blasphemy. She taught me how to make a good cup of tea.

Tea 101

> *"To make tea properly, have the water at a rolling boil. Don't even think about a microwave. Use a good teapot and pour a bit of the boiling water in and swish it around—warming the pot. Dump it out. Use a good strong tea (loose or in tea bags) and fill the pot with the boiling water. Allow it to steep for a few minutes. Get out a nice china cup and saucer, milk, never cream, and sugar if you like. Tea always tastes better in a china cup. And one more thing, saucers. Some people seem to think saucers are fancy or just for decoration—oh no, they're very practical. They are almost like a little table. A place for a tea bag or you can tuck a biscuit in them, drips are no bother, and it makes it easier to hold a nice hot cup. Mugs are great, but if you have a teacup, please don't forget the saucer. It's a sin."*

Mrs. Kelly's Journey Home

Mary Kelly loved to travel. Though she never learned to drive, she really got around. She was always open to new experiences—I always said she'd go to the opening of a donut shop. She kept her precious U.S. passport up to date, and though she never learned to drive, she really got around. She was good company and enjoyed people. After her camping trips to Northern Michigan with the Wilsons, she expanded her world at every opportunity.

One day, Mrs. Wilson suggested they go on a "girls' trip" with her cousins to the Bahamas and invited Mary to join them. It was just seven days, but it was an exotic location, and Mary was all in. They took a trip on a glass-bottom boat, though Mary had a terrible fear of water. She brought home a very large, very dead starfish, and my prized possession was a small, square woven handbag with flowers and *The Bahamas* embroidered on the lid.

Her Irish friend Bernadette Kenney lived in Toronto and traveled throughout Canada selling antiques, primarily fine sterling silverware. She invited Mary to travel with her for a summer from Toronto to British Columbia in Bernie's van. She didn't need to be asked twice. I was in college, and my younger brother John stayed with our brother Donagh and his wife Sue while Mom was gadding about across Canada for a few months. Life with Tom Kelly was not easy, and I believe these little trips with her girlfriends were necessary for her mental health. Respite is essential.

Her trips to Ireland were as frequent as she could manage—about every five years or so. If there was a family wedding or a funeral, she found a way to go. On one such trip, her sister Lillie had organized an excursion to Malta and she was able to add another stamp to her passport. In the 1980s, Mary decided to accept an invitation from her brother who lived in Cape Town, South Africa. She saved up, booked the flight by herself to London, then to Johannesburg, and then to Cape Town. It was a fabulous adventure and she loved sharing the stories of her travels. She really was very brave.

Tom Kelly was a man of great wit, and I thought of him as a crusty cupcake. Rough on the outside but sweet and soft on the inside. He had a few tender favorites—grapes and balloons. Whenever anyone was feeling unwell in our home, he would go to the store and bring home a container of fresh grapes. Every time. He believed they had "medicinal properties." Actually, just this small, gentle act of kindness had the medicinal magic. He also thought every party or celebration was incomplete without balloons. He would bring home a small plastic bag of balloons and we would spend an afternoon blowing them up and then taping them to the walls of the basement before any special occasion. Not a Martha Stewart look, but it was festive.

Tom Kelly had the gift of pessimism, especially when it came to change. My mother, the eternal optimist, made a great foil for his caustic remarks. He had a knack of finding the downside to pretty much anything. After I moved out, my parents decided it was time for new windows in the little brick house. My mother wanted new windows that had decorative muntins (white crossbars) and my father wanted clear windows—no muntins. This argument went on for weeks. After the windows were finally installed, I popped over to take a look. By this time, I knew who I was dealing with, and whenever I visited, I played a mental game of waiting to see how long it would take for my father to make a negative remark about something. He never disappointed. I'd been in the house less than ninety seconds when I asked him what he thought about the beautiful new windows, with muntin bars. He replied, "You know what it looks like from the inside, don't you? Prison bars!" He was masterful.

As difficult as he was, he was a generous man. Whenever he came to our home for a little visit, he usually brought a small gift, a carved wooden bird or an ornament. Once, it was a large German beer stein. He would place it somewhere (unwrapped) on the mantle or a bookshelf and then wait. After a bit, he'd ask, "Did you notice anything?" I would then stop whatever I was doing and have a look around and hunt for his treasure. I usually took my time to find it so he would get some satisfaction with his little surprise. All kinds of wild things ended up in our home. He probably bought them on the street in Detroit or from a guy at the bar selling things out of a big suitcase.

Mrs. Kelly's JOURNEY HOME

Peggy (Kelly) Walsh visiting the west of Ireland

Tom and his sister Peggy were two peas in a pod. Peggy lived in Dublin and worked as a housekeeper for the neighborhood church. A widow, she cooked and cleaned for the priests living in the rectory, but she had the Irish irreverence and scorn for authority down pat. She never referred to her employers as "Father" or "Reverend." She always called them "the auld bastards." Probably to their faces.

In addition to being a skilled master printer, Tom was also very interested in social justice.

He became active in the union for printers, The Detroit Typographical Union #18, and ran for office. He worked in the Free Press as the Union representative for more than twenty years. With his intelligence, skill, and gift of gab, he was often asked to go to the "other side" and join management. He declined every opportunity. His heart was with his union brothers and sisters, and he couldn't be swayed. I remember many union strikes when he had to go to Toledo to work as a printer for months. He never crossed a picket line. At one point, he decided to leave his job as a printer in the composing room at the Free Press and become a full-time officer of the DTU. He spent several decades as the secretary/treasurer, serving the union members and especially taking care of the "old age pensioners." Many a weekend afternoon was spent visiting his pensioners and seeing how he could help them. He was a proud Irishman and an even prouder union man. I remember one Saturday afternoon standing on the picket line with him in the 1960s supporting Cesar Chavez's grape boycott at a local grocery store.

Tom Kelly at a Typographical Union Convention

A large portrait of President John F. Kennedy hung proudly in our little home, right over the small buffet displaying a few pieces of Waterford Crystal and remnants of Nelson's Pillar in Dublin. Nelson's Pillar was a landmark in the center of Dublin honoring the British Horatio Nelson. It was scorned by Dubliners and was ultimately blown up in 1966. Tom proudly kept a chunk of the pillar as a symbol of freedom. My parents were so proud of the first Irish-American Catholic President and were devastated after Kennedy's assassination in 1963. Mary was pregnant and exactly one month later, she delivered a healthy baby boy. They named him John Fitzgerald Kelly, JFK. Mary didn't want him to be called Johnny, so he was referred to as J.F. for most of his childhood. Some Americans thought his name was Jeff, just pronounced with two syllables.

In 1968, my father attended a union rally in Detroit featuring Sen. Robert Kennedy, the Democratic candidate for president. As a leader in the union for printers, Tom got the chance to meet Sen. Kennedy and brought a portrait of his young son, JFK, with him. He asked Sen. Kennedy to sign the picture and he obliged. Just three months later, he too was gone. Our nation mourned and our family grieved, again.

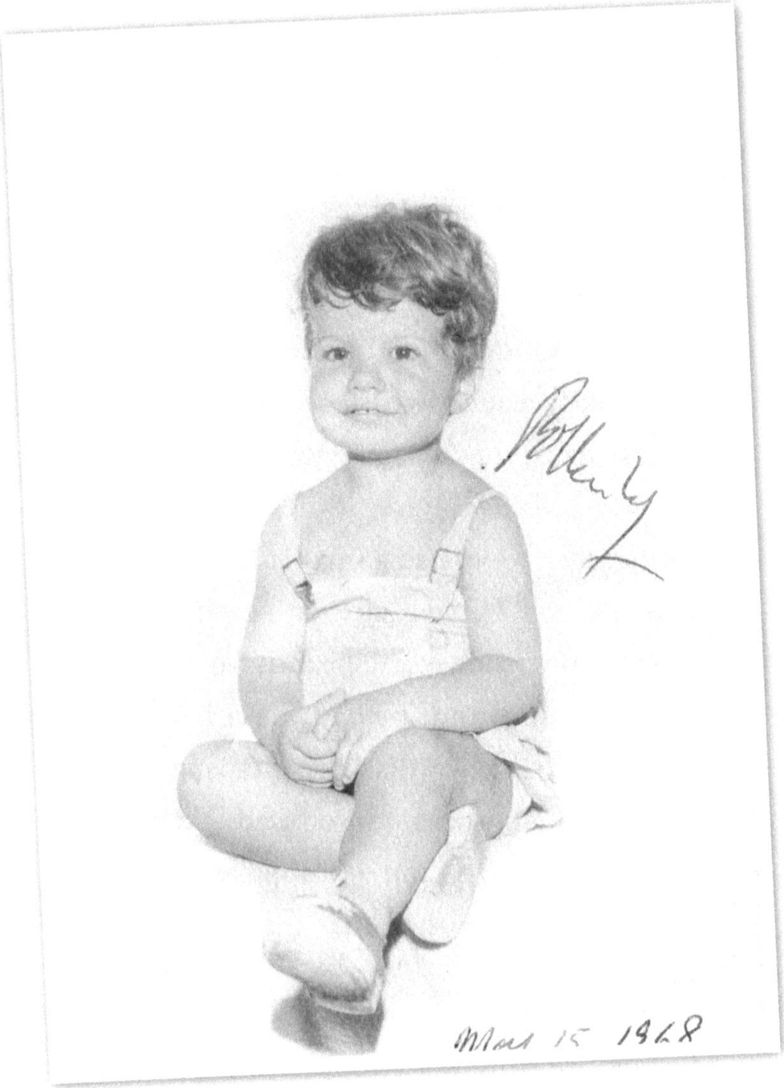

Portrait of John Fitzgerald Kelly autographed by Senator Robert Kennedy, 1968

Tom Kelly was far from perfect, and he experienced many challenges. The day the union office was robbed at gunpoint in Detroit and the office staff was herded into the single bathroom with the door locked, he thought they would be executed. The experience changed him, and I don't believe he ever recovered. He retired soon after that and was never the same.

He received his pension in one lump sum, and he and Mary made a few trips to Ireland. On one of those trips, they stayed with his sister in her 200-year-old row house. It didn't have central heating; each room had a small fireplace. Except the bathroom. He told me that he would never forget his first shower the next morning. It was cold and damp, and the bathroom had only a cast iron tub with two separate taps, a rubber hose, and a hand-held shower head. He had become Americanized and was appalled. He said, "I've pissed harder than that shower…warmer too."

His favorite store was Montgomery Ward. He loved that store. We called it Monkey Wards. After he retired, he needed a small lawn mower and asked my husband, Jim, to go with him. In the store, the salesman asked if they needed any help. He said, "Just let me know if you and your son have any questions."

My dad just smiled. In the parking lot as they loaded the new mower into the car, he said, "Did you notice I didn't correct that fella about you being my son?"

He bought my mom a diamond ring as she had never had one. He instructed me to select it, however, because he said, "It'll be yours one day and I want to be sure you like it."

My mom had only requested that it be an oval-shaped stone. We worked with a local jeweler, and she chose a chunky gold setting with six prongs that would keep the stone secure. I was never a fan of the setting she chose. After she died, the ring became mine. I immediately thought of getting a new setting for the beautiful oval diamond, but I had no idea what I wanted. I decided I would first get the ring resized to fit me (her fingers were tiny as well) and choose a new setting later. As soon as I had the ring sized to fit me and I tried it on, I couldn't believe how much I loved it. It is perfect and I wear it every day. A very precious gift from my father and my mother.

Mrs. Kelly's Journey Home

Mary and Tom Kelly on the dance floor at the Gaelic League

Tom Kelly never trusted doctors and was proud of the fact that he never went to one. He chain-smoked Pall Malls, and the only exercise he ever got was getting up from his chair to walk to the fridge for another beer, Carling's Black Label. Whenever my husband went to their home to help with some household repair, my dad would watch him work and then announce that he felt the need to take a nap. He was exhausted from watching Jim work.

Retirement didn't suit him. He had lost his purpose. One day in 1993, he told me he wasn't feeling well, and I offered to take him to a doctor and make sure they didn't do anything he didn't want. He shook his head and told me, "No. I'm not able to go to the doctor. I'm not feeling well enough. Besides, they'll want to do those invasive procedures, you know, the blood pressure test."

Just about a week later, early on a Sunday morning, an aneurysm burst in his heart. He was still in bed. Mom called 911, but he was already gone by the time they arrived. She called me, and I drove in the rain the fifty miles to their home. I turned on the radio and "Tears in Heaven" by Eric Clapton was playing. Before I left the house, my five-year-old son Daniel asked me if Papa was sick. He then asked me if I was going to hold his hand. When I arrived at the hospital and saw my father on the gurney, I took his hand in mine and told him we loved him so.

When my mom, my sister-in-law Sue, and I cleared out my father's closet, we discovered the pockets of his favorite Irish cardigans were filled with paper-wrapped Starburst candies. I had told my dad one day that our kids loved them, and they took a while to eat because they had to unwrap each one. He'd stocked up and now we knew one of the reasons the kids followed him everywhere. Tom Kelly wasn't an easy man to understand or live with. He did his best for us and he loved us all.

> **Tom Kelly Quotes**
>
> *Holy Christ Tonight!*
> *I am sure Mrs. Wilson did it.*
> *I'm just telling you…*
> *I ate it, didn't I?*
> *She's a real bidula.*
> *Here come the banticles.*
> *Could I get a side plate?*
> *Is it union-made?*

Mrs. Kelly's JOURNEY HOME

Tom Kelly in Wicklow, Ireland, 1990

A Tribute to Tom Kelly

By colleague and friend Don Lewis, 1993

Thomas J. Kelly. Is 1,000 words too much?

Tom Kelly's heart quit beating Sunday morning, May 23, 1993. It is believed he was taken quick, without pain, perhaps to have him linger as a sick man—would have been too much.

He had too many loves to count. But these were his dearest: his family, his union, and his country—and there were two, Ireland and America.

Mrs. Kelly's JOURNEY HOME

Tom Kelly and Don Lewis in the Detroit Free Press Composing Room, 1960

Tom Kelly loved the linotype machine a bit too much. When he first worked at the Detroit Free Press, his fingers stroked the keyboard of the linotype machine like a pianist playing a concerto. His Irish eyes sparkled with delight as he demonstrated "hanging the elevator" to a young apprentice. The Chairman lectured, "Too fast. Too much."

Tom Kelly loved politics a bit too much. When first he involved himself in the politics of the Detroit Free Press Chapel (union), he worked the room like a born politician, smiling, eyes blazing with the joy only an Irishman can project when in a good fight. He was elected, served as Chairman for 17 terms. Some of those served said, "He wins too much."

Tom Kelly loved fighting management too much. When Chairman of the Free Press, he took great delight in verbally battling any foreman who gave a "God-fearing union printer nuthin' but a hard time." During those years, he told a young journeyman, "A printer, if nuthin' else, should at least get an 8-point obit. And I don't think that's askin' too much."

Management, at that time, said no man working the line in any factory gets such recognition. It's too much. There are those, still today, who read a printer's 8-point obituary and say, "He (or she) was only a printer. Isn't this a bit too much?"

Tom Kelly, upon leaving God's green earth, got his 8-point obituary and might have said, "Sure, and for what more can a man ask than a newspaper's 8-point obit for working at something he loved?" Still, he might have asked, upon reading his obit, the same question he once asked about his campaign literature: "Do you think it's a bit too much?"

No, Tom. Not this time. Too much of what you did for too many has never been told…too much.

Do you remember this incident, Tom? As Secretary-Treasurer of the Detroit Typographical Union #18, you once called a young Chairman at the Free Press and told him one of the printers, off sick, "should be in the Printer's Home…and, by Jesus, I'm gonna get him there."

"Tom, you told me the other day, there's no room. There's a waiting list."

"No room at the Inn, but Jesus Christ was born, wasn't he? Well, we'll see what happens." You laughed. "Maybe they have a stable."

And your Irish laughter echoed through the line even after the "click" signaled the end of the conversation.

A couple of hours later, a printer—with no family, no money, owning nothing but a frail and failing body— was on a flight to Colorado, to the Union Printer's Home. You personally put him on that plane, Tom, knowing they wouldn't send him back…the ITU would find room at the Inn.

You taught that young Chairman a lesson still remembered: for those who are down with nowhere to turn, a fellow human being can never do too much.

You might had too much dedication, too much pride in we who worked as printers, and you may have fought too hard to get too much for many of us who still think we didn't get enough.

Do you remember contract negotiations beginning at nine a.m. and breaking at 2:30 a.m.? That was too much.

Tom, do you remember spending Father's Day, among days before and after, isolated in a hotel, separated from your family, trying to negotiate a contract? You were not alone there, but some of the others said, "Maybe we're asked to give too much."

Some were exhausted, but you told jokes, one after the other into the wee hours of the morning. During those breaks between sessions with the publishers, your Irish humor was needed. Nothing that eased the tension and stress was too much.

There's talk of tearing the old hotel down, Tom. It's useless, has been for some time. Anyway, you, Tom, left us before that old building. But useless you were not. You were retired but still giving your

time to the Union…unpaid. You never thought it was too much.

Some said you talked "Unionism" too much. Your close friends knew how to switch your conversation: just ask a question about your family. Ah, the Irish grin would split that Kelly mug and it was as if a leprechaun had magically turned you from union advocate—arguing vehemently—into a loving husband and father, filled with pride and boasting a wee bit too much.

You must know, Tom, that your daughter, Breeda, thought you were a very religious man…you attended so many Chapel meetings. Surely you know that Brendan said you instilled in all your children, David, Donagh, and John, a work ethic, so much so that he doesn't dwell on rumors about plant closings. Endowed with that work ethic, he doesn't worry too much.

Your family, from the youngest grandchild—was ten too much? No—to your beloved Mary will be fine. Sure, there's a time for grieving, and maybe when she sees to it that you join forever with the water in Dublin Bay, you'll be goin' with a few of her tears, but Lord, Tom, asking her not to shed a tear…wouldn't that be expecting a bit too much?

We'll all join you eventually. Would ya mind seein' there's room for us all? Is that asking too much? Tom Kelly—Tommo to your closest—you gave too much to ever be forgotten. You'll be missed…too much.

Mary, Breeda, and Tom Kelly, 1959

In the morning as I waited for the school bus, my father would often tell me stories. One fall morning, he told me about the month of November. He said it was known as the coldest, dreariest month of the year. Dark and gloomy, the trees were bare, and everything looked dead before the beauty of the winter snow arrived. I was near tears as he described this dystopian world, my world. Then he got the sly Tommo twinkle and told me that one day, in the middle of November, a bright light shone. It was a glorious day filled with sunshine and warmth, right in the middle of the bleakest month. Because a little girl had been born to brighten this dark and gloomy month. He laughed and smiled as I began to giggle and ask, was it November 16th? He said yes, indeed it was. My birthday, the brightest day in November. Tom Kelly was a man with a brilliant mind, strong opinions, and a heart of gold. He hid this last bit very well under a caustic and crusty exterior, but I knew who he really was.

Unlike my brothers, I embraced my Irishness. I took Irish step-dancing lessons and attended events with my parents at the Gaelic League in Detroit. We attended competitions called Feis', and my mother taught me a few poems in Irish, the ones she had learned as a child. I was never RiverDance material, but my recitations in Irish were well received. My favorite was a poem called "Misha Raftery." It's about an elderly man lamenting his lost youth. I learned it phonetically and had no idea what I was saying. Apparently, I got it right. I won a medal for that one.

Mrs. Kelly's JOURNEY HOME

Breeda Kelly at a Detroit Feis, 1967

Mrs. Kelly's Journey Home

My mother wanted me to take Irish step-dancing lessons and the only place available to us was the Gaelic League in Detroit. Every Saturday morning, we took the bus from our home all the way into the city. It was about a forty-minute bus ride. We got off at the massive Detroit Post Office and then walked about a mile to the Gaelic League, passing Tiger Stadium and many shady bars and pawn shops. We were often able to hitch a ride with another family to return home in the afternoon, but it was never a set plan. Mary Kelly didn't drive, and asking Tom to drive into Detroit after working all week was not an option.

Thirteen was a big year in my life with events that would shape my future. That summer, my mother had scrimped and saved to take a summer holiday in Ireland with me and my younger brother, John. Transatlantic fares were very dear and money was tight, but she did it.

By now, my parents had become naturalized U.S. citizens, and this was her first trip using her crisp new U.S. passport. We stayed with her brother Ronnie's family in Dublin, and for four glorious months, we lived in Ireland. My aunt sent me to the butcher shop up the road for a pound of "mince." I had no idea what that was. Turns out it was a pound of ground beef. The butcher was a friendly chap and when he heard my American accent, he told me he had a cousin in California and wondered if I knew him. I explained that I was from Michigan and that California was pretty far away, so no, I didn't know his cousin.

We spent the summer visiting cousins, aunties, and uncles, and my only living grandparent, my Granny Kelly. We traveled to the West of Ireland, and I rode a horse on the beach. The horse decided to go for a swim, and I was terrified that she would wade deep into the Atlantic and I'd never be seen again. Fortunately, she decided to turn around when the water reached my stirrups. I made loads of friends and even considered going to boarding school in Ireland. I loved it.

When we returned home in the fall, things took a very serious turn. I developed severe pains in my abdomen, so my mom took me to our local doctor. She didn't drive and had no car, so we went to a doctor within walking distance. She had no choice. He examined me and sent us up the road to a specialist, about a half mile away.

We walked. He examined me and performed a small surgical procedure and sent us home.

The next day, I developed a raging fever and had severe pain. Mary asked Mrs. Wilson to drive us to the doctor's office as it was over a mile away. Then she called Tom at work to meet us there. We were confused and very scared. With no family and few friends, it was a very difficult time for my parents. I sat in the doctor's private office with my parents as he explained what was wrong. Then to my horror, he drew a picture of the female anatomy in front of us. My father was beside himself, twitching for a cigarette. As soon as we got outside the office, he muttered, "I don't need to know all the details, just take care of her, for Christ's sake. Mary should know about these things. She's a woman. This is horrible for me!" Yes, yes, it was horrible for all of us. I was taken to the local hospital and admitted.

I developed a mysterious infection in my abdomen, likely from contaminated instruments in the doctor's office. This led to four surgeries, six weeks in the hospital (two of them in an isolation unit), discussions of colostomies and hysterectomies and my last rites. I nearly died. The doctors didn't have a clue and were throwing everything at me to see what could get rid of the beast, the infection, within me. I survived and I thrived. Not in spite of this experience but, I think, because of it.

At this early teen age, I matured very quickly. I watched the adults around me. I saw bad behavior and I saw deep, abiding love and optimism. I experienced great personal care at a community hospital that by today's standards would be considered third world. But the nurses were simply the best. I was the mystery kid in the end room who always said "please" and "thank you," and, when there was no end in sight, tried to keep other's spirits up. I was my mother's daughter.

The gift of nearly dying at such a critical age was something I didn't appreciate at the time. I could have done without drainage tubes coming out of my gut and daily blood draws. To this day, I cannot stand the tourniquet on my arm for blood draws. I hate the needles, too, but that rubber strip strangling my arm still freaks me out.

I will never forget sitting in my bed in the ward (I had been sprung from the isolation room when my fever finally broke) and hearing my team of doctors walk down the hall. "We have no idea what cured her. We gave her enough antibiotics to sterilize a stallion." I just smiled. I didn't care. I felt like myself again. It was the day before my fourteenth birthday, and I was going home. I had missed eight weeks of eighth grade, probably why I never did well in math—algebra was introduced, and I missed the important bits. But I had learned so much more.

- Adults don't know everything.
- Keep trying new things if things don't work out.
- Be gentle with families of sick people.
- Always say please and thank you—even to the guy who draws your blood and uses an arm tourniquet, every day.

I learned these lessons at thirteen. I have never forgotten them, and they have served me well. When I think back to those dark days in the hospital, I was the lucky one. I was unconscious most of the time. I had no idea how seriously ill I was. My poor mother was beside herself with worry. My parents had emigrated from Ireland just fourteen years earlier and she'd never learned to drive. I had four brothers, and my father loved his family, but he loved his beer as well. Every day, my mother had to find a ride to the hospital to be with me and manage my brothers at home. My young brother, JF, had to sit in the lobby of the community hospital for hours because children were not allowed on my floor. John was eight and had no idea what was happening to me.

Mary also worried about how Tom was handling this crisis. Not well. I was his only daughter, and he adored me. His method of coping was to go to the bar after work every day and then make his way up to visit me. I loved the fact that he loved me and was worried about me, but I dreaded his drunken visits when he would sit on the side of my bed and cause the mattress to sink, which pulled my sutures and bandages. He didn't stay long and I don't know if anyone else knew he was loaded. But the child of an alcoholic recognizes that glassy-eyed look and fierce attempts at sober behavior, not to mention the stench of Carling's and Pall Mall. To this day, excessive alcohol and cigarettes are my least favorite things.

The nursing staff became my second family during my six-week stay. In fact, the head nurse—Nurse Harvey—was my champion and my savior, and I called her my other mother. Her care for me in the most frightening and uncertain of times gave me hope and gave me confidence that everything was going to be okay.

Once I was out of isolation, I was given a roommate with an unknown illness. All I remember about her was that she was a big fan of "Big Time Wrastlin." She was ultimately diagnosed with Hepatitis after sharing my room and bathroom for three days. This required *me* to get the shots to prevent myself from coming down with her illness on top of my own situation. The nurses drew straws to determine who would have to inflict the painful gamma globulin injections. They agonized over this additional injustice, but in the end (my end), they held my hand and administered the painful shots. When I said, "Thank you," they burst into tears and told me what a good job my mother had done raising me.

If I hadn't had this experience at age thirteen, I might not have had the gumption to put myself through college—the first one in my family to do it. I might not have had the courage to attempt the things I had no business doing and then end up either learning a great lesson or being successful. I learned that stuff happens to everybody, and it truly is how we respond to the bad things in our life that determine our quality of life. I am always learning new ways to do things differently and to do them better, and I love that. I haven't always followed these lessons, but I come back to them and they are my truths. My mother taught me by example through her optimism and her faith.

After I recovered and was released from the hospital, I went back to junior high school and life went on. Had this happened today, there probably would have been a lawsuit, but my parents were just grateful I was alive. They didn't understand the legal system here and didn't know what might have been the right course of action. Being an immigrant presented so many challenges. Little did we know how this event would impact the rest of my life.

Breeda Kelly as The Maid of Erin, 1976

When I was seventeen, I met Jim. We went on a few double dates with a mutual friend and his brother. The first time he met my father, at the Gaelic League in Detroit, he introduced himself and mentioned that he was dating me. It was the night of the Maid of Erin (Queen of the Irish for the St. Patrick's Day parade) contest, and I was getting ready to go on stage. My father shot him a dagger look and then Jim thought he'd make a bit of small talk. He mentioned that he drove an MG, and that the car was made in Great Britain. My father paused, took a long drag from his Pall Mall, and stated curtly, "I fail to see the greatness." My dad got over the idea of his daughter having a boyfriend and Jim's unfortunate word choice. My parents loved Jim and considered him a fifth son.

Mrs. Kelly's JOURNEY HOME

Ellen Cullen and Mary working at the Irish-American Festival, Detroit, 1975

My mom and her best Irish friend, Ellen Cullen, instructed me early in life, "Never marry an Irishman!" It was common knowledge, and they drilled it into me, daily. They had good reason. While their husbands were charming, they had very old-fashioned ideas about marriage and they enjoyed their drink a bit too much.

That summer, I traveled to Ireland on my own. The prize for winning the Maid of Erin contest (Queen of the Irish in Detroit) was a trip to Ireland (for one), and I was thrilled to see my cousins, friends, aunties, and uncles. I was less thrilled about a solo visit with my Granny Kelly, my father's mother, Anastasia Cullen Kelly. I had met her once before with my mother when I was thirteen. She scared the living daylights out of me. To say she was severe would be a compliment. The best way I could describe my grandmother was my dad in a dress with a white curly wig and a large mole.

Anastasia and Thomas Kelly, 1979

Mrs. Kelly's Journey Home

She was not a warm, cuddly grandma then and I didn't have hope that she had changed. I stayed with my mom's side of the family and visited the Kellys.

First up was my dad's sister, my Auntie May. She greeted me with a hot cup of tea and a warm hug. It went downhill quickly. The minute I sat down, she pounced. "Are you going to marry an Irishman?" she asked.

My reflexes kicked in and I responded automatically, "I'd never marry an Irishman."

She nearly spilled her tea. "Sure, they're the finest men on the face of the earth!"

I tried to recover. "Oh yes, I just mean I haven't met any nice ones yet."

She wasn't having it. "Aren't they all grand?"

I muttered something and focused on my tea. Soon it was time to head over to Granny Kelly's house. Thanks be to God.

Mrs. Kelly's Journey Home

As we approached the solid row house in Marino, I saw her standing in the doorway. She didn't smile as Auntie May introduced me. "Ma, this is Breeda from America. The cheek of her! She says she'd never marry an Irishman!" Then she turned on her heel and left me alone on the doorstep. I offered my hand as a greeting with a faint "Hi." She clearly wasn't a hugger. I followed her into her dark sitting room. It was small and every square inch was covered in framed photos of her children, grandchildren, and great-grandchildren.

She showed me photos of my dad as a young man and even one of me in my First Communion dress. My mother told me that Granny Kelly never liked children though she had nine. Could be why. It was a hard life.

I was only in the house a few minutes when she looked me right in the eye and wagged a gnarled finger. "I spent me life raising babbies," she announced. "Don't you spend your life raising babbies."

I just gulped and nodded. My uncle was picking me up at three and it was only two p.m. I was in survival mode. I pulled out my envelope of family photos to have something to talk about. My parents, my brothers, our house, our dog…and a photo I had meant to remove. My handsome, blond boyfriend, Jim. I was only seventeen and didn't know if she would approve.

Jim Miller, age 22, 1976

She studied all the photos and asked lots of questions. When she got to the picture of Jim, she stopped. No one in our family was blond. "Who is this fella?" she asked.

I stammered, "That's my boyfriend, Jim."

"Hmmm, he doesn't look American."

What did that mean? I responded weakly, "Well, his family is of German heritage…"

She squinted and looked at the photo for a long time. "Is he a good man?"

I smiled. "Yes, he's a very good man. We've been dating for six months."

She looked at the picture, looked at me, looked at the picture, and looked back at me. Then she poked the photo and announced, "Marry that fella!" She went from warning me against spending my life raising babies to telling me to get married, all in under ten minutes. I had whiplash.

That was forty-five years ago. I don't remember what else we talked about that afternoon, but when my uncle came to collect me, I gave her a big hug and she hugged me back. I didn't know my grandmother, but apparently, she knew me. I took her advice.

My engagement ring was a beautiful gold Claddagh Ring, a traditional Irish engagement ring. It's a gold band with a heart held by two hands and a crown on top. It symbolizes love, friendship, and loyalty. It has no diamond or other stone. When we had it made by a local jeweler in Detroit, my friends didn't understand how it could be an engagement ring without a diamond. It was and it is. On our wedding day, my wedding ring was my grandmother's (my mother's mother) wedding band. A slim platinum band with five small diamonds in a row. It was like new, not worn or thin as most rings of that age might be. My mom gave it to us in the original box from a Dublin jeweler. She explained that her mother kept it in the box on the top of her dresser and only took it out each Sunday to wear to Mass and then returned the ring to its safe home. That's why it seemed new and unworn. I had it sized to fit my (larger) finger. I love the history of this tiny little ring.

Mrs. Kelly's JOURNEY HOME

Mary & Thomas Kelly, Breeda and James Miller 1984

Jim and I married after many years together. We wanted to start a family and that is when we began a journey we never planned. Infertility. Because of what happened when I was thirteen, the doctors said our chances of conceiving were very low due to scarring from the infection and surgeries. The lessons I learned helped me deal with the infertility I experienced as a result of this illness. It was a huge disappointment to learn that one of my greatest desires was just not going to happen and that I had to figure out what to do about it. The light bulb went off when my husband and I asked ourselves a key question: What was our goal? To achieve pregnancy or become parents? We answered that question and hopped off that roller coaster quicker than you can say hysterosalpingogram. Be grateful if you don't know what that is. Our family was built through adoption and as the saying goes—my kids didn't grow under my heart; they grew in it.

We began by calling a local adoption agency. We were told that due to Jim's "advanced age" (he was thirty-five), by the time a baby became available, he would be too old. It turns out this was not true, but we didn't know any better and just believed them. We then turned to international adoption and after a year of ups and downs, forms and reference letters, and even getting fingerprinted for an FBI check, our son, Daniel James Miller, arrived from Seoul, S. Korea, on June 17, 1988. He was a sweet, four-month-old bundle of joy and had Jim's hairline.

Daniel James Miller, 6 months, 1988

Mrs. Kelly's JOURNEY HOME

The day we got the call to go to the airport to meet our first child was very special. After waiting so long, it was hard to believe. The only tangible thing we had was a photo of the baby sent by the adoption agency in Korea. I made copies of this precious image and shared them with our family. Everyone gathered at the airport to meet the newest member of the clan. Jim and I arrived at the airport hours early, waiting anxiously. We saw my mother walking toward us in the concourse and noticed she had something stuck to her shirt. I really hoped it was intentional. As she got closer, we saw that she had taken the photo of our baby, cut it into a circle, and pinned it to her shirt like a badge. She said she wanted to be sure that Daniel knew who his Nana was. The circle was complete. It was the immigrant welcoming the newest immigrant home.

Daniel with his Papa, 1988

Chloe Kelly Miller arriving in Detroit, 1991

A few years later, our beautiful daughter, Chloe Kelly Miller, arrived from S. Korea on November 21, 1991. My dad called her Beeswing too. Our family was complete with the arrival of Evan Thomas Miller a few years later.

Mrs. Kelly's JOURNEY HOME

Both Daniel and Chloe arrived home to us at four months of age and traveled to Michigan with an escort from South Korea. When we applied to the adoption agency for our third child, we requested a toddler and were open to a child with medical issues. Evan was nearly two years old and was born with a cleft lip and palate. He had a few other issues and because he was a bit older (nearly two), we decided that I would travel to Seoul to bring him home myself. We thought it might be better to meet his foster mother (babies awaiting adoption in South Korea live with foster families, rather than orphanages) and travel on the long flight home together.

My journey to Seoul was eventful. Leaving Detroit Metro Airport on that April morning in a freak blizzard, we sat for four hours while the plane de-iced. The flight itself was direct and took thirteen hours. I watched six movies. I arrived in Seoul after midnight (their time). It was a holiday weekend, and all the hotels were full, so the adoption agency had found a host family that I could stay with during my short visit. All I knew was that I was staying with Dr. Park, no phone number, no address. Seoul is a large city with a population of more than 10 million. Park is one of the most common surnames. I was terrified, and the words to my favorite hymn kept replaying in my head, "Be Not Afraid." I had no idea how I was getting to her home. The agency just told me that someone would drive me there.

As I emerged from the double doors in the baggage claim, there were crowds of people waving and waiting for their families and friends. *Be not afraid.* I scanned the crowd and then I spotted him. A tall, thin Korean man with a small white sign that said, "Mrs. Miller." I nearly jumped out of my skin and waved frantically at him. His expression never changed. He waved me to follow him to the parking lot. It was the middle of the night, and he spoke no English. He led me to his white van. I got in. All I knew was that I was supposed to go to a private home.

I had no idea how large of a city Seoul is. We drove for nearly two hours and were still in a very large, very crowded city. Suddenly, he took a sharp turn into an alley and stopped in front of two large, carved wooden doors. I thought this was the end of the line for me and not in a good way. *Be not afraid.* He hopped out of the van, swung open the doors, and unloaded my very large suitcases (filled with donations for the adoption agency). The wooden doors opened, and there in the moonlight stood two women. One spoke English, and she embraced me and welcomed me to her home. She was Dr. Park, and she led me through her courtyard to a small, private apartment.

Evan Thomas Miller, age 3, 1996

Mrs. Kelly's JOURNEY HOME

My visit to Korea was short and memorable. The next morning, Dr. Park invited me to walk with her up the mountain. Her home was built into the side of a mountain in Seoul, and I saw Koreans practicing Tai Chi in the park. Then she took me to a public bathhouse, which was quite an eye-opening experience. Suffice it to say that stripping down and bathing with a group of nude strangers was a memory I won't forget. She was a doctor, and I did what I was told. I was the only Caucasian in a bathhouse filled with naked Korean women; I'm sure it was memorable for them as well.

That afternoon, I took the subway to the Korean adoption agency to meet our new son. He was so sweet and happy, giving big hugs and sloppy kisses. I had created a laminated picture book of our family and our home and sent it earlier, so he might recognize me. The flight home was interesting as he slept for only twenty-two minutes of the long flight and pushed every button he could find. The Korean flight attendants scolded him in Korean, and he settled down for a bit. To say I was exhausted after this journey is an understatement. Our house was full, and our family was complete. Who knew that the children we were meant to have would be born to three different women on the other side of the world?

Mrs. Kelly's JOURNEY HOME

Our family was complete. Chloe, Evan, and Daniel, 1995.

Mary Kelly in her element with her grandson Daniel on her lap, 1988

When I worked at the radio station, my mother cared for Daniel and she loved every minute of it. I would bring him to her early in the morning, and she saw how excited he got when the garbage trucks came around each week. So, every Wednesday morning, she would strap him into his stroller and head out the door to follow the truck through the neighborhood, so he could see the process up close. The fellows on the truck would wave to him, and he was thrilled. One day, a neighbor stopped her and asked, "What is he?"

My mother gave her a sharp look and said simply, "He's a beautiful baby boy and he's my grandson!" She turned on her heel and went on her way. A prouder nana one would never find.

Evan, Chloe, Nana, and Daniel

Both of our sons have learning disabilities. They work very hard every day to keep up. In school, they received great opportunities. They attended special education classes and also were able to integrate into general education classes. When Dan was in seventh grade, he was in the regular social studies class. He had many friends in school, most of whom were scholar athletes, and they really looked out for him.

One day in class, there was a trivia contest, and the room was divided into two groups. The score was tied and the final question was asked: "What was the middle name of President John Kennedy?" Daniel's arm shot up, and everyone in the class turned to look at him. No one knew the answer. He confidently responded, "Fitzgerald!" and the class erupted in a spontaneous cheer. His teacher was so delighted she phoned me at home that evening to relay the story. Who knew that having an uncle named after a former president would create such a wonderful moment?

Nana and Chloe at her baptism, 1991

My mother and our daughter Chloe had a very special bond. She was her princess, and they were very close. When Chloe was about six, she asked me why Nana always said "Mercy Flower" when she was worried about something. I had no idea what she meant. I repeated it several times, Mercy Flower, Mercy Flower until it hit me—my mother was saying "Merciful Hour." It was a shorthand version of the prayer, "Merciful Hour of sweet Jesus, please save us." The two of them were like peas in a pod. Baking together, reading books, and sharing secrets. When Chloe was baptized, my mother presented her with the same delicate silver Claddagh bracelet I had as a child. Watching the two of them play on the big swing on the old willow tree outside my kitchen window is one of my fondest memories. We took a trip to Ireland with our kids and Mom in 1998.

Chloe, Mary, Jim, Evan, and Dan in
Brittas Bay, Ireland, 1998

Mrs. Kelly's JOURNEY HOME

The Miller Family
Evan, Dan, Breeda, Jim, and Chloe
2024

Mrs. Kelly's JOURNEY HOME

Onward.

After Tom died, Mary lived on her own for the first time in her life. She was still in the little brick house across the street from the Wilsons. It's about fifty miles away from the small town where we lived, and I would drive in each week to take her shopping. She enjoyed our little village and longed to be nearer to her grandchildren. But that meant leaving her little brick house after forty years and leaving her dear friend, Virginia. That was the hardest part. Raymond Wilson had passed on a few years earlier, and Virginia had her son Mark and Mary Christina still at home. As we were loading up the moving van, Mrs. Wilson said, "Cripes sakes, it's the end of an era."

Mary sold the house and bought a charming little condo just a mile away from our home. She was a spry seventy-five, and for the first time in her life, she chose everything. She even painted her bedroom walls herself. Tom had been the painter and never let her touch a brush. My brothers (and sisters-in-law) all helped fix it up, and Jim even installed a little fireplace for her. She loved it. She embraced our village, walking the mile to our home frequently. She took yoga classes and attended the senior luncheons. Our kids would stop in after school for a special snack. Life was good.

Mary and her brood: Donagh, Brendan, David, Breeda, and John. Jim is appearing magically in the photo in the background, 2008.

Mary and Tricky Woo at her condo, 2005

Part 2

A NEW JOURNEY

It was early November 2006. The fall colors of Michigan were still hanging on and it was beautiful. We had been chatting on the phone when Mary had a violent coughing fit and collapsed. Jim was home, and we rushed her to our local hospital. We took her to the ER, thinking it was a migraine headache gone very bad. She had suffered from severe migraines most of her life. It's a condition that I too experience. Not all hereditary characteristics are welcomed.

She was treated with some pain medicine and released from the hospital into our care. She was not herself, and the next day we had a visit to a new doctor (her regular physician had recently moved out of state). She was diagnosed with a strained back ligament and told to take two Aleve tablets.

We took her to our home because we didn't want to leave her alone in her condo. She was extremely restless and agitated. During the night, she got up out of the bed in our guest room five times and collapsed on the hardwood floor—despite my having barricaded the bed with pillows. I stayed on the couch all night to be near her.

At six a.m., I heard a creaking from the door to our basement, which was next to the bathroom door. I thought it was our son going downstairs to play video games. Then I heard a sickening tumble and crash to the floor. Fifteen steps down a wooden flight of stairs to a cement floor—my mother lay in a heap. As Jim and I flew down the steps, she lifted her head and asked softly, "Am I bleeding?" I said, "No, you're not." I asked her to move her limbs and her neck and then asked if she wanted to go back to bed. She said yes. We helped her up and she was able to put her full weight on her legs. With our help, she walked up the stairs back to bed. She had made a wrong turn out of the bathroom and opened the basement door, thinking it was the guest room. She had been diagnosed with osteoporosis a year ago but only suffered a small bruise on her back and not so much as a broken fingernail. Jim installed a latch on the basement door immediately.

To be safe, we took her back to the ER where they did a CT scan of her brain and found a cerebral hemorrhage, which likely occurred during the coughing fit. She was taken by ambulance to the University of Michigan Hospital in Ann Arbor, where a wonderful chief neurosurgeon met us and looked after my mother personally. His parents were Irish immigrants as well. That night, she was admitted to neuro-intensive care and our saga really began.

The type of brain bleed she suffered (an AVM) was small (of course it was) yet very rare in its location within the brain. She remained in intensive care for ten days and underwent two cerebral angiograms (under general anesthesia), an MRI, three CT scans, and a full cardiac workup. We all knew that she had a big heart, but it was good to hear it was healthy as well. She was very frail, and we were all worried. My four brothers, Jim, and I waited anxiously to hear what the doctors had to say.

Troops of doctors came to analyze and discuss options. Due to her age—she was seventy-eight—no one was in a hurry to perform open brain surgery. In fact, Dr. Thompson said to me, "Your mother deserves a thoughtful decision." Wiser words were never spoken. He said he would like to delay a decision and allow her to gain some strength and be in a better position to withstand whatever treatment would be determined. We agreed.

She was due to be released by the neurosurgeons when she developed a bit of a "plumbing" problem and had to undergo an unplanned surgery to repair a prolapsed bladder. As she was being wheeled into the OR, she said to me, "I could do without this!" Couldn't we all? She came home with a catheter in my care to build up her strength for the impending brain surgery that was scheduled for one week before Christmas.

We saw the neurosurgeon to discuss his plan for the surgery. He told us the risks and the options of a radiation treatment that was less invasive but would not eradicate the problem of the blood pooling in her brain. The best option was to surgically correct the malformed blood vessel and remove the residual blood in her brain stem. To be certain of the location and size of the problem, he wanted to do one more angiogram (her third) under general anesthesia and then have her spend the night in the intensive care unit under observation. Then they would operate to repair the damage to her brain.

Thursday morning, Mary Kelly went to the University of Michigan Hospital to have more dye pumped through her arteries into her brain and have photos taken. At about four p.m., the host at the Family Surgery waiting room called me over to take me back to the recovery area to see my mother. She told me cheerfully that my mom was all set and I could take her home. I followed her back into the recovery room with my brow furrowed, very concerned. She was supposed to be heading up to Neuro Intensive Care, not heading home.

Mary Kelly was sitting up with a big grin on her face and a sparkle in her eye when she announced, "They say I'm cured and I can go home! It's a miracle! I'm blessed!" My mother's faith is very strong, but even this was a bit much. I patted her hand and told her to lie down and enjoy the anesthetic. I had to find the doctor. This made no sense at all and I was very confused.

The doctors were flabbergasted. They said they had never seen anything like this before. After the dye was injected and the cameras were rolling, they found no evidence of a damaged blood vessel and no blood pooled in her brain. It was completely normal. I asked if this happened very often. The doctor said it was extremely rare—and her problem was rare in the first place. Less than 1% of these cases resolve on their own. Her brain surgery was canceled. He also suggested we might want to buy a lottery ticket on the way home. This was our lucky day. Perhaps it was a miracle.

I bought Mom this game that Christmas. I told her it was the only Brain Surgery she was going to get.

Mom recovered, but she was not the same confident, independent woman. She had no paralysis, but her spirit was shaken. She moved in with us, as her sweet condo was a tri-level and there were too many steps. We made room for some of her furniture. Jim built a special shelf for her precious collection of teapots. He put up grab bars and rails and even built a porch level with the house so she could get outside easily. Our old farmhouse had a first-floor bathroom and a bedroom. It was perfect. We wanted her to feel at home. But sometimes I really got it wrong. I was so busy doing all the caregiving things. Meds, appointments, schedules. I sometimes missed what really mattered.

Mary with her ever-present cup of tea visiting in Georgia

Mom lived with us and took her last breath in

her own bed. She recovered from the stroke, but she wasn't herself. For about two years, she was able to travel to visit my brother and his family in Georgia, and they loved having her with them. I would escort her on the flight down and she especially enjoyed spending time with her grandsons. Her eldest grandson, Connor, organized a special tour of his school, The University of Georgia, and procured a wheelchair so he could take her to see everything on campus. She loved every minute of it.

Mary and Sir Toby Kelly, 2000

Years later, she got a Yorkie to replace her very active Cocker Spaniel named Tricky Woo. Yes, she was a fan of All Creatures Great and Small.

Tricky Woo loved to chase after squirrels, and he was dangerous on a leash. We feared he would take her down and decided to get her a tiny dog. Tricky Woo went to live with Donagh and his family. This new little fella was five pounds of love. Sir Toby Kelly was her constant companion, and he was a sweet dog.

Mom loved being in our home with all the kids and dogs. Toby was always at her side. She even created a song and would sing with great enthusiasm. Daily. There are few things in life that would drive me to distraction, and that song was one of them. When we had visitors, she told them Toby had a song and asked if they would like to hear it. I think they thought the dog was going to start singing or something. They were captives and had to listen—to all the verses. I had to leave the room. Mom often commented about how I got so many "client calls" during the day…

> *"Toby Kelly, Toby Kelly is the best little doggie in the world (bum bum)*
> *Toby Kelly, Toby Kelly is the best little doggie in the world (bum bum)*
> *Toby is my little fella! I love him so, don't you know?*
> *Toby Kelly is the best little doggie in the world (bum bum)"*

The Long Goodbye

In time, she developed dementia along with a number of other age-related ailments. After a lifetime of high blood pressure, her heart was growing weaker. She developed congestive heart failure and then vascular dementia. I didn't know what I didn't know. I had no training; all I knew was that I loved my mom. I spent my days being torn between my kids, my husband, my work, and my mom. I had never felt so frustrated, exhausted, and isolated. No matter what I did, I felt I was letting someone down. Her dementia would come and go, and when she was in the fog, life was hard. She wasn't always this way. Mary Kelly was a sparkly little Irish lady with big green eyes who sprinkled herself with Estee Lauder's Youth Dew like it was holy water.

They call it The Long Goodbye. Dementia. I missed all our great chats and trips together. Mom was happiest when she had booked a trip and loved to travel—I can't recall her ever saying no to an adventure. But now, things had changed, dramatically. Dementia is kind of an umbrella term and there are over 100 types: Alzheimer's, Lewey Body, Vascular, and others. Some are worse than others, but they are all heartbreaking. Dementia really is the long goodbye.

I learned so many new terms. I've always liked sandwiches, but this was something else. I was now a member of the Sandwich Generation. It's when you are caring for a generation on either side—your mom or dad, as well as your kids. And you are squeezed in the middle. Just when you are done loading strollers into your van, you're loading up walkers and wheelchairs. I lived in the Caregiver Sandwich for nearly six years. Three young teenagers and a mom who was declining.

My mother kept me on my toes, especially at doctor visits. Whenever we met a new doctor, she always had an opening statement. I would brace myself and cringe when she began. I sat behind her and often made faces at the doctor while she answered their questions. She announced, "I've been blessed. A miracle. I'm not like other people. I'm very petite and you cannot give me the regular doses of medicine because I have miniature organs."

I was so embarrassed and would just shake my head. But then I realized I couldn't change her behavior and maybe I should start enjoying it a bit. I began to look forward to the doctor's reaction. I would wait to see their expression and response to this tidbit. I looked for any way I could to lighten up my day. When my mother was having a hard time sleeping, a geriatric specialist told her she should stop drinking tea. She was appalled at the very thought. "You might as well tell me to quit breathing." She did, however, begrudgingly agree to begin drinking decaf tea. When we had a follow-up appointment a few months later with the same doctor, she opened her handbag to show me what she was taking with her. It was a single decaf teabag in a little cloth pouch. She told me she was going to shove this in the doctor's face. When I told her that I didn't think that was necessary and he might take offense, she muttered something and put it back in her handbag. She didn't take it out at the appointment, but she gave me a side eye when the doctor asked about her tea-drinking habit. Never a dull moment.

We were very fortunate to have an extraordinary primary care physician for Mom. She was a great listener and even made house calls. At one of those calls, she sat knee to knee with Mom in her favorite chair and explained that Mom's pain from neuropathy was not curable but could be managed with medication. She also looked her right in the eye and told her that her congestive heart failure was not going to get better, but that she would do everything she could to help her. Her direct, honest, and kind presentation of this information was appreciated by my mother and by me. Mom accepted this, and though she was still opposed to taking "all those pills," she was a bit more cooperative. For a while.

Mom had arthritis and her doctor recommended ibuprofen. When she complained about the pain, she often refused to take those "mind-altering drugs." I was so frustrated by her refusals that I called her doctor, who simply told me to tell my mother that if she refused to take the pills that would ease her pain, then she wasn't allowed to talk about it anymore. I told Mom what her doctor said and she agreed to take the ibuprofen. It never ceased to amaze me what would work to solve caregiving challenges. At this stage, caregiving was like a day at The Improv. I never knew what I would be dealing with, and it required creativity and patience. Neither of which I had in large amounts anymore.

I wish I could say that I handled every situation with humor and grace. Some days were better than others. I was the only daughter with four brothers, the default caregiver.

Her dementia got worse. It would come and go. Some days she would be sharp and herself, and other days she would be anxious and disoriented. Vascular dementia is like that; it's all about the blood flow into the brain. Alzheimer's disease is different; the decline is consistent.

One day, she announced: "You're an alcoholic and I'm leaving. I'm going to Georgia."

I was shocked at the accusation and responded that I couldn't be an alcoholic because I don't drink. Without missing a beat, she responded sharply, "Denial!! That's the first sign."

I was devastated. My father was an alcoholic. I was upset and called my brothers, who thought it was hilarious. The next day, she was fine and never mentioned it again.

She often thought there were two Breedas and would complain to me about the "Bad Breeda" who would make her take mind-altering drugs—like Advil. One time, she was pretty cranky and demanded to see both Breedas.

She summoned me to her side and said, "I want to see both Breedas in here at the same time. I don't want to have to repeat myself!"

I responded, "But Mom, I'm here. You know there's only one Breeda."

Then she snapped back, "Oh, is the other Breeda too busy on her computer to come in and talk to me?"

I thought I might lose my mind.

Pills were a daily topic of discussion. Mom was not a fan of medication and could not swallow the big "horse pills." She had nicknames for many of her pills, especially the ones she disliked. She had strong opinions, and it made caring for her challenging.

Prescription drugs are expensive, and I was always on the lookout for ways to save money. One day, I was at our local pharmacy and had a little chat with the pharmacist. He told me that one of Mom's prescriptions was now available as a generic. This would offer a significant savings opportunity. I knew whom I was dealing with though and needed to set the stage. I knew that generic drugs often came in different shapes and colors from the brand name. This could be a problem. Mom had had a recent experience with a different, new drug that came with terrible side effects. It was an oval blue pill. So, I asked the pharmacist to show me the new generic ones. They were small, round, yellow ones. I went home and shared this cost-saving news with Mom. She seemed pleased and then asked what color the new pills were. I told her they were yellow. She smiled and said, "Oh good. Yellow. Those are the good ones." I smiled and hoped that the manufacturer wouldn't change anytime soon.

Some days were better than others, but it was always a challenge. My brothers lived out of state, but they were very involved and I was grateful for their long-distance support. They called her weekly and visited as often as they could. I appreciated their help with paperwork, finances, and major decisions. I realized they couldn't help her use the toilet or give her a shower even if they lived nearby. As she declined, her ability to travel great distances was lessened, and her visits to them were no longer possible.

After living with us for two years, she fell and broke her hip. When it comes to hip fractures in the elderly, this is often the beginning of the end. Mom had osteoporosis, and I understand that it's unknown whether the bone breaks and the person falls or if they trip (or are dizzy) and fall and then the bone breaks. Regardless, it was an unwelcome and difficult next phase. She had hip replacement surgery and then spent six weeks in a nearby rehab center. If I'm being honest—it was the best six weeks of sleep I'd had in years. But with hospitalization and weeks in the rehab facility, her dementia worsened, as often happens with elderly patients.

Mom returned home to us with a walker and became incontinent. I had no experience dealing with this new challenge. Was this normal or did we need to see the doctor?

We had a physical therapist who came to the house to continue her treatment. Daryll was a kind man, and Mom looked forward to his visits. She had a hard time but would persevere. She proudly reported to him how many "laps" she had taken around the kitchen island with her walker. Mom was terrified of falling again and would stay safely in her chair for much of the day. She was very clever and decided that she could avoid the stress of getting up to use the toilet if she didn't drink much. So, she refused to drink her water, and her tea consumption was noticeably reduced.

Then I discovered another wrinkle—she was having "accidents." I placed waterproof pads and towels on the furniture, but it was not a solution because she invariably chose the seat without protective layers. I loved my mother, but I was worried about my new couch—you know, you can only flip the cushion once. After one session, I asked Daryll if he had any advice. He told me that people who use disposable underwear have fewer falls. What? That seemed like a very odd statement. And what would using disposable underwear have to do with falling in elderly frail folks? First of all, I had never heard of calling adult diapers "disposable underwear." And it didn't occur to me that Mom should be wearing them. It's not a normal topic of discussion and I didn't know if it was a medical problem or just a normal part of aging.

Daryll explained: "'Disposable underwear' is a respectful term that doesn't embarrass or diminish adults like calling it a diaper does. Most falls happen when older adults are in a hurry to use the toilet. This can cause anxiety and then rushing, often resulting in tripping over the threshold in the bathroom. By wearing disposable underwear, there is no fear of an 'accident' or a need to rush. Therefore, there are fewer falls among older adults."

After Daryll left, I casually mentioned to Mom what he had shared with me. Mom's response was simply, "Can we get some of those?" Let me just say I have never left my house so quickly to head to our market for a big, pink package of disposable underwear. I emptied out her underwear drawer and replaced all her panties with neat little rectangles of disposable underwear. We never discussed it again. I realized that sharing the information in this way allowed Mom to be part of the solution and to request this new idea, rather than being told what to do. She was able to keep her dignity, and my couch was saved.

Our kids loved their Nana and were a great help. Chloe spent a lot of time with her, and they had great chats and many cups of tea together. Dan was always available to get whatever was needed and was very patient with her. Evan was simply extraordinary. When Nana would get up from her chair and use her walker, he was always there to "spot" her and make sure she didn't fall. Mom had a dental bridge and was constantly taking it out and tucking it into various spots around the house, between cushions, and often inside her pillowcase. We spent many a morning searching for Nana's teeth. Evan was brilliant at finding them. I don't know how, but he was the expert at finding the missing bridge.

For nearly six years, our big old farmhouse was a hub of activity. We were remodeling and adding space, our kids were becoming teenagers, dogs were constantly underfoot, and Mom was declining. Jim worked the night shift and needed to sleep during the day. It was a very challenging time but also one filled with amazing life experiences and love. Lots of love.

Jim found time to renovate our old house and built a new family room and a life-altering screened porch. The addition of this screened porch cannot be overstated. It added a living space that allowed us to enjoy the outdoors in comfort. When he built it, he made sure that it was level with the floor in the house so that Mom could get out there easily without navigating any steps. When we initially discussed her moving in with us, she was very concerned about her precious teapot collection. In her condo, they were displayed in her little dining room. With all the activity in our home, she was worried that they would be in danger. Jim solved this worry by building a shelf near the ceiling around the perimeter of our dining room as a safe way to display her teapots. She could enjoy looking at them and not worry about any accidental damage. One less thing to worry about.

Our kids were involved in school sports and driver's training, and had loads of friends. It was hectic and the years flew by. I worked with a small company that enabled me to have a home office. That way I could look after the kids and my mother. I often joked that I had the worst of both worlds…I never got to leave. Between scheduling appointments for my mother and my boys, who had medical issues, it was a lot. I spent my days juggling my responsibilities and feeling guilty regardless of how much I did.

One of the biggest lessons I learned was that to maintain my sanity (which was hanging by a thread), I needed to lower my standards and appreciate the concept of trade-offs. What I thought was important was changing as I adapted to the daily onslaught of requests and demands. I knew it wouldn't last forever, but in the moment, it was hard to comprehend and accept my limitations. I came across a tiny souvenir plate from Ireland that had these words imprinted on it:

> *Our House*
> *It's clean enough to be healthy*
> *and dirty enough to be happy.*

It was exactly what I needed, permission to give myself a break.

Mom was moving much slower and her walker worked fine around the house, but when we needed to go places, I realized she needed something more. The idea of using a wheelchair was something I had not yet considered. I wanted to retain my mom's dignity, but I also needed to be able to get her out and about without exhausting her and spending an eternity waiting for her to walk through a store. I knew next to nothing about home medical equipment. All I knew was that it was expensive, heavy, and usually gray. It also had a stigma attached. I didn't want to have my mom feel like she was an invalid. Using a wheelchair might have a negative impact on her mental state. Then I stumbled upon an ad for a small, lightweight wheelchair called a transport chair. Unlike all the gray and institutional-looking wheelchairs I was familiar with, these transport chairs came in some pretty snazzy colors and designs. A wheelchair as a fashion statement! Yes, this might work.

I had mentioned to Mom that the Detroit Institute of Arts was having an exhibit featuring the work of Norman Rockwell, one of her favorite artists. But she said she wouldn't be able to walk through the museum and let out a big sigh. A light bulb went off in my head. I said, "Mom, I saw an ad for a new kind of wheelchair called a transport chair. It's small and lightweight and I bet we could find a pretty one. What would you think if we got one and then we could go to the museum to see the Rockwell exhibit?" Her face lit up and she said that would be a lovely idea.

I began shopping for a transport chair that would suit Mom and our budget. I found a lovely plaid chair (not unlike a Burberry plaid), and she loved it. It was lightweight and I could load it into my car. The day we went to the DIA, she was thrilled, and I found a plaid scarf that matched her new chair. People stopped her to compliment her on her lovely chair and matching scarf, and she beamed. Mom never felt diminished by using the transport chair, and it allowed us the opportunity to go on many more adventures. Her favorite store was T.J. Maxx, and we often went on retail therapy excursions. One time, she asked to go there, and as we headed into the store, I asked which section she wanted to go to. She said, "I don't want to tell you." I was pushing the wheelchair, so I had to know what she wanted. She then clarified, "I want to buy you a present, but I want it to be a surprise for you." I'm not sure how we navigated that excursion, but I remember how deeply her little plan touched my heart.

Mrs. Kelly's JOURNEY HOME

A visit to the Detroit Institute of Arts, 2009

Delirium was another thing altogether. Delirium is different than dementia and can happen for lots of reasons, such as dehydration, UTIs (urinary tract infections), and sundowning. Sundowning is a change in behavior that occurs in the late afternoon or early evening. Confusion, increased agitation, and often periods of delirium are exhibited during a sundowning episode. I had never heard of it and it was a terrible surprise. One minute, Mom was herself and the next minute she was extremely agitated, shouting and crying. Hospital stays and anesthesia are thought to be culprits as well. For a new caregiver, this bizarre behavior was not only unwelcome, but it was also terrifying. We never knew how long an episode of delirium would last and we did everything we could to help her feel safe while it lasted. The primary cause was dehydration, and it was a daily struggle to get her to drink more fluids. Apparently, the sense of thirst diminishes as we age, just when your body needs hydration the most.

I wasn't doing a great job taking care of myself because I was so busy taking care of everybody else. I was cranky and short-tempered. My kids often told me I needed to take a nap. The exhaustion was building; my frustration was overwhelming.

It was Thursday. Shower day. I hated giving my mother a shower. It was so stressful. She was terrified of falling and I wasn't trained to do it. I hadn't been sleeping. Mom was calling out for me. I had changed her bedding three times that morning. My phone was ringing off the hook. I was late with a proposal for a client. The dog threw up on the carpet and then at four p.m., sweet Evan simply asked, "What's for dinner?"

"What's for dinner?" I cried out. "What's for dinner?" I ran into the bathroom and slammed the door shut. I leaned against the wall and sank to the floor, thinking, *I can't keep this up. If I don't find a way out, this is going to kill me. I don't know what to do. I'm not cut out for this. I'm a terrible daughter and a worse mother. I can't do this anymore. I didn't sign up for this, I don't know what I'm doing. I'm exhausted. I can't keep going like this. I need help!*

I reached out to friends, and one suggested I consider hospice.

"No," I responded. "She's not that bad."

I thought hospice meant death was imminent.

But my friend gently explained to me that hospice is much more. It's all about comfort care, and they could provide services that would help me care for my mother, probably at no cost. I had no idea. I called a local hospice organization and made an appointment for a nurse to come and meet with us.

The hospice nurse showed up with all the papers from Mom's doctor, and we sat and chatted. Then it was time for the big introduction. My mother was nothing if not practical and never wanted to be a burden to me. That helped me break the ice, but it was hard. She was having a good day and was up and alert. "Mom, this is Margaret. She is a nurse with hospice and they are going to help me care for you."

Mom extended her hand to greet Margaret and then stated brightly, "I'm delighted to meet you. I know all about hospice. You're a great group. I'm not ready to croak yet, but I'll take all the help I can get." I wish I had a photo of Margaret's face.

The very next day, medicine was delivered to our door along with a giant box of disposable underwear. Then the home health aide came and gave Mom a shower. That alone was the greatest gift. I think hospice saved my life. This was July. Many people experience a surge of energy and seem to rally and get stronger when they enter hospice care. I think it's because the pressure to get better and measure success is simply gone. It didn't last very long, but it was wonderful all the same. The focus is on comfort and providing calm support to the family and person in care.

By the fall, Mom was becoming more and more frail. She was seeing people who weren't really there, sleeping most of the time, and becoming upset very easily. The hospice nurses said we might not have her much longer.

My mom wasn't a fancy cook, but we were always well-fed—especially when it came to her baking. She could make scones and soda bread with her eyes closed. Her brown bread was legendary. But it was her pie—her apple pie—that was her claim to fame. The smell of her apple pie would bring our neighbor, Mr. Wilson, to the side door for a fresh, warm slice. When she became a U.S. citizen, she made a huge concession to America by turning her traditional Irish apple tart into an all-American apple pie by adding cinnamon to her recipe. It was a big deal.

But as she became frail, she needed a walker to take a single step. Her balance was so poor she couldn't manage the simplest tasks. When she couldn't even make herself a cup of tea, she said, "I'm just Useless Eustace."

We knew we wouldn't have her for much longer, and Thanksgiving was more than a month away, so we planned a big family get-together in October. My brothers, who lived in different states, would come with their families and we would celebrate together. The reality of this was that I would not only have to take care of Mom, but I would also have to entertain and feed all of them as well. Picture this: we have a big, old, creaky farmhouse, three teenagers in various stages of immaturity, two dogs, my husband working nights, and I have a pesky day job, working from a home office—while caring 24/7 for my eighty-five-year-old mother, and we decide to have a big family dinner. What could possibly go wrong?

My brothers were excited to visit and called Mom to tell her they couldn't wait to see her. Donagh told her he couldn't wait for a taste of her delicious apple pie. And that is when things went south.

From that moment on, Mom never stopped asking when we were going to make the apple pie for the boys. Every day. All day. Never mind that I had my hands full getting ready for visitors. The truth is, I don't do pie. I didn't inherit my mother's hand with pastry. The few times I have attempted to make a pie have not ended well. There was a lot of cursing and the final product was gray and tasted salty, from my tears. My kids can tell you exactly what a conniption looks like. They've seen it.

I called Donagh. "What were you thinking when you told Mom you were looking forward to her pie? Are you nuts? You know that means I have to make the pie—she can't make a pie anymore. And she is so worried about you guys and your piece of pie, she won't let it go." Donagh said not to worry—he would bring a pie. And that calmed Mom down. For a bit.

So, the big day arrives. I have the table set with Mom's Waterford Crystal, her good china, and an Irish linen tablecloth. Mom is asking about making the pie again when in walks my brother with a pie. In a white cardboard box. With a clear window. With Kroger printed on the side and a big orange sticker that added insult to injury—"half off." My mother was appalled and refused even a bite of this "store-bought pie." And when he told her it was just like her pie—well, she might have dementia but she knew apple pie. Fortunately, we were able to divert her from "piegate" and the day ended well.

They all left, and I was wiped out. The next day as I was packing up her good china, crystal, and linens, Mom asked about making the apple pie. The party was over, but she couldn't let it go. It became an obsession. Apple pie. I'd be loading the washer and hear the rumble of her walker in the hallway and then I'd hear her. "Are we making an apple pie today? The boys love my pie. Did you get the good apples? Apple pie today?" Well, it pushed me right over the edge. I was the poster child of a burned-out, stressed-out caregiver. I thought I was going to lose my mind. If I heard apple pie one more time—that would be it. For the first time in my life, I realized I needed professional help or I might go before her.

So, I got the name of a counselor and made an appointment. He asked why I'd come. I started in with my list of complaints. How much I had to do, how busy I was, how much pressure I was feeling, how little sleep I was getting, and how hard it was *taking care of everybody.* I told him how my mom was relentless in asking about making an apple pie. I told him the party was over, there was no need, and that I don't do pie. I'm not good at pie. I don't even like pie. It was unreasonable and unnecessary. It was making me crazy.

He was such a good listener. I knew he'd be supportive. Tell me that I was right. That I needed to set boundaries and that this was just an unreasonable request. He set down his notepad and pen, leaned forward, and said, "Breeda, you gotta make the damn pie. Pick a date, write it on the calendar, get the ingredients, and tell your mom you're going to make the pie with her. Then just do it. You won't regret it."

I wasn't happy about his response, but I did as I was told. I chose a date, wrote it on the calendar, told Mom we were going to make a pie, and got all the ingredients, including "the good apples." The day arrived. I put an apron on me and one on Mom. She was able to sit at the counter and we began.

Mary Kelly with her paring knife, November 2010

I handed her her favorite wooden handled paring knife—she didn't believe in apple peelers. Her magic fingers used to make one long, curly ribbon of peel—but now, even though she couldn't do that, she got that look in her eyes. I remembered how those magic fingers of hers were able to make big curls, ringlets in my long, brown hair, and set them with bobby pins and almost a full can of Aqua Net hairspray when I was five. I peeled the rest of the apples and sliced them just so. She directed me. Mary Kelly would not be rushed.

As I handed her the cup of sugar, our fingers touched, and I remembered the time I watched her make pie when I was in Junior High and didn't make the student council. She said to me, "Your ship will come in one day." I handed her the wooden spoon, and she gave the apples a good stir. I did my best to follow her directions with the pie dough. I pushed the rolling pin back and forth, and she gave it a few good slaps. There was flour everywhere—on the floor, the counter, the dough, the dog, and me. I looked like the Pillsbury Doughboy.

I managed to wrestle the slab of dough into the pie plate. Mom and I took turns placing the perfectly spiced apple slices, just so. She had taught me so much. I remembered how she instructed me to point my toes and hold my arms loosely at my sides when I practiced Irish step-dancing, just as she had been taught in Dublin. I trimmed the top crust of the pie, and she asked for a scrap of dough and the little knife. She cut out three leaves and I placed them in the center of the crust. The aroma of the apple pie baking was intoxicating. We admired the beautiful pie, and after it cooled a bit, she was able to eat a few bites along with a nice cup of tea.

She wore a look of pride on her face as we sat at the table together. Then she announced it was the best pie she'd ever made. She was delighted.

I was so ashamed. I had been so consumed with doing all the things, following the schedule, and being busy. I forgot what really mattered. And I was so very grateful to be called out before it was too late. To do what I needed to do. Listen to what my mother really needed and make time for it. It was never about the pie. It was about making the pie. Sometimes, you just gotta make the damn pie.

In early December, Mom made a special request. She asked me to find a priest to give her the Last Rites, or the Sacrament of the Sick. This is a sacrament in the Catholic Church intended to give peace and grace to the gravely ill. Mom wasn't a fan of our local parish priest. So, I called a parish in the next town and asked if the priest would make a house call. It was a large parish and we didn't know him personally. He had a packed schedule, but he agreed and said he'd be over on Tuesday morning, early. He arrived before eight a.m. It was snowing. He was in his seventies and looked very tired.

I greeted him at the door, and he reminded me that he wouldn't be able to stay long as he had a very full schedule. Then he asked me if Mrs. Kelly could take Holy Communion. I thought this was an odd question, and I told him that I didn't think she had committed any sins lately. He smiled and said that he meant to ask if she was still able to swallow. Embarrassed, I said yes, she could.

I led him into her room. She was in bed with her arms folded over her chest and her eyes closed. It was very odd because she'd been up earlier. I made the introductions and Fr. Will took out his blessed oil, stole, and crucifix. He was about to begin the sacrament when she interrupted him.

My mother asked from her prone position, "Now hold on a minute, Father. I have a question for you before you begin. Do you know what this sacrament was called…originally?"

Fr. Will looked up at her and responded, "Why uh, do you mean Extremunction?"

After a long moment, my mother smiled and said, "Yes, that's very good. You may proceed."

Fr. Will got a big smile on his face and told her that his grandmother was Irish. I left them to do some work at my desk. An hour passed and they were laughing and talking. As he got up to leave, his entire manner had changed. I thanked him for coming and asked if he would pray for my mother. He responded, "For Mrs. Kelly? Oh, no, she'll be fine, she's all set. *You*, I'll pray for!"

Mary Kelly was always comfortable around death. When her sister-in-law May was diagnosed with terminal cancer, there was no one able to stay with her and care for her. So, my mother packed her suitcase and stayed with her in Dublin for four months as her caregiver. Before she died, Auntie May bequeathed her beloved dog, an ornery, spoiled Yorkshire Terrier named Ben, to her. It was her dying wish that Ben go home to America with Mary. So, she took him, of course. That dog was known as "the little shit" and the "Yorkshire Terrorist." His favorite activity was to lift his leg and piddle a few drops on the sleeve of anyone unfortunate enough to leave their jacket hanging on the back of a chair. No matter what he did, my mother's response was, "He was a legacy gift." Toothless, blind, and bossy, he lived the good life in America for many years. Auntie May would have been pleased.

Politics was always a topic of discussion and action in our home. Mary and Virginia were active in many campaigns, and my mother was very proud of being a trained poll worker for a few years. When a local woman was running for statewide office, she embraced my mother and the two became good friends. Loretta Moore's unfortunate cancer diagnosis cut short a promising political career, and she asked my mother to be with her at her home during her last days along with her hospice team. Mary Kelly's sunny disposition and matter-of-fact approach to the end of life was a comfort to so many. I learned so much from her. She taught me how to live and she taught me how to die.

In addition to family, many friends stepped up to help. Our friend Joan came up with a brilliant plan to visit Mom every Tuesday afternoon. Joan loved my mother and they both enjoyed an Irish television program called *Ballykissangel*. It's a sweet drama series set in a small village in Ireland. Joan would go to our library and borrow a CD of the series, and she would sit with Mom and enjoy the program together. It gave me an hour to myself—to catch up on work or maybe even take a nap. It was such a lovely and thoughtful gift of time. They both enjoyed their visits together, and the lighthearted series set the tone. Mom belonged to the village Senior Citizens group, and through them, I found a woman who would come over each week for a few hours as a companion to Mom, so I could leave the house to run errands or just go for a long walk. We paid her and she was a great help for several years.

When Mom needed hospice care, I was initially hesitant. I had no idea of the range of services and support that hospice provides, and I certainly didn't know that Medicare typically covers all the costs of hospice care. This was a revelation. I learned that hospice care is all about comfort care and that many people are able to receive care for months. My mother was under hospice care in our home for seven months, and the care she (and our family) received was extraordinary. During that time, we had regular visits from nurses, home health aides, a chaplain, a social worker, and even a volunteer professional photographer to take a portrait of Mom. Medicine and supplies (including disposable underwear) were delivered to our door. All at no cost to our family. I truly believe hospice saved my life.

**Mary Kelly and her cup of tea.
portrait courtesy of Arbor Hospice**

Mom grew weaker. She had some good days, but they were few and far between. It was December and she was anxious. She said she was going on a journey and needed her suitcase, her good one. I asked her where she was going and she said she didn't know, but that she was going somewhere. I got her suitcase and left it next to her chair. She never put anything in it, but it seemed to calm her, just having it nearby. Then she called me to her side.

She told me that she wanted to go home. That she needed to go home and wanted the bus schedule to Dublin.

I tried to change the subject, but she kept asking. Every day. One day, I was so frustrated I even tried to explain.

I said to her, "Mom, the buses from Michigan to Dublin are not very reliable, and how would you climb up into the bus?"

She was determined and stated, "Oh no, they've gotten much better and the conductor would help me."

She was relentless and I was exhausted. One day, she was sitting in the family room wringing her hands. She was very upset and near tears. I asked her why she was so upset. Then she told me,

"It's that Breeda. She's horrible. I keep asking her for the bus schedule and she just won't get it for me."

Something clicked in my head, and I said to her, "Mom, don't you worry about that bitch. I'm here today and I'll figure it out."

I had absolutely no idea what to do. I couldn't actually take her to Ireland; she was too frail to travel. She couldn't even leave the house at this stage. What would help her? She loved to travel. She was always so happy after she had booked a trip. Hmmmm. What if I made her a ticket? I googled "fake tickets," and in seconds, a template for a fake boarding pass popped up. So, I started to fill it in. Departing airport: DTW. Arriving airport—this was tricky. I could put in DUB, but I thought I'd go one better. Hmmmm. What about HEAVEN? Departure date: Open. First Class. Yes! And it was an American Airlines boarding pass. My brother John worked for American Airlines, and my mother was very proud of him and told everyone. This was perfect. I found some card stock and hit "print."

Mrs. Kelly's JOURNEY HOME

Boarding Pass

Class / Classe: FIRST CLASS / PREMIÈRE CLASSE			Name / Nom: KELLY, MARY P
Flight & Date: Open	Gate: A12	Seat: 26B	Seat & Class: 26B A
Boarding time: 01.00am			
From: DTW	To: HEAVEN		To: HEAVEN
Name: KELLY, MARY P	Airline use: 0081A	AAC27670	Remarks: Mrs. Kelly's Journey Home

I walked over to Mom's chair and handed her the boarding pass. "You don't have to worry anymore, Mom. You're good to go."

She studied the card, smiled, and exclaimed, "Oh! This is great! I'll show this to Father Will!"

Over the next few weeks as people came to visit for the last time, instead of being anxious and worried, she was excited to show them her pass. "Wait 'til I show you what Breeda got for me!" They all had a good laugh and told her she was, indeed, blessed.

I've witnessed a few miracles in my life, and I believe that finding that boarding pass online and seeing the delight in my mother's eyes was my favorite. She never asked about the bus schedules again, and she kept the pass nearby until the day she died.

On her last New Year's Eve, we spent it in her room watching Bette Midler in concert. I decided to make it as festive as possible, so I found two sparkly crowns and magic wands, and we had a great laugh making wishes and being silly.

Just eleven days later, she took her last breath. We sat with her at her bedside, though she could no longer speak or communicate. On Sunday evening, a dear friend stopped by to check on us. I took a break, and we sat in the living room, adjacent to her bedroom for a chat and a cup of tea. After about ten minutes, her beloved Yorkie, Toby, ran out of her room and started barking at me. I got up and walked the few steps into her room. She was gone. Her labored, shallow breaths were no more. She was at peace, and I was shocked at my reaction. I wasn't overwhelmed with grief. I was too tired to cry. And I felt enormous guilt for the relief I felt for her and for me. Then I realized that I had been grieving for years. Six years, for the vibrant Mom I knew and loved so much. Dementia is the long goodbye and I had been saying goodbye for years. Now, I knew she was at peace, and I could remember the woman who was so extraordinary. She could be herself again.

Mrs. Kelly's Journey Home

The Irish have a wonderful relationship with death. An Irish Wake is the original Celebration of Life. I grew up listening to my parents and family having the most hilarious conversations about dying, death, and beyond.

- When my Uncle Vinno, a very dapper and witty man, was diagnosed with lung/brain cancer, he consoled those who were attempting to console him. "Sure, aren't we all in the departure lounge? Some of us are just a bit nearer the gate!"
- My Aunty Peggy (my dad's sister) criticized her widowed sister-in-law for taking ballroom dancing lessons. "She should be at home praying for a happy death!"
- My dad and his best friend Owen Cullen argued over the best spot to be buried. Owen wanted to be buried on the Hill of Howth because of the great view. Tom responded, "What do you care about the view? You'll be six feet under." Many years later, after Tom died and was cremated, my mother carried his ashes back to Ireland and he was buried in the Kelly family plot, at the Hill of Howth. I really wanted to plant a plastic periscope at the gravesite for him. I know he would love it, though it might freak out other visitors.
- A favorite Irish Blessing: *"May you be in heaven a half an hour before the devil knows you're dead."*
- Ten years before she became ill, my mother wanted to make her final arrangements. I reluctantly went with her to the funeral home to make the plan and then made the trip to the local cemetery so she could choose her spot. She did not want to be buried in Ireland; she said America was her home now. She carefully chose

Mrs. Kelly's Journey Home

a spot on a hill and was delighted to see who her neighbors would be—they included a former Governor and Supreme Court Justice of the State of Michigan, John Swainson. She found joy in just about everything.

It was my final gift to her to create her headstone. I researched and agonized about the style, design, and wording for months and shared my ideas with my brothers. After many versions and options (too many, I'm sure), my brother David told me, "Just pick one! It's not cut in stone." Actually, it was.

Mary Kelly, resting in peace, Manchester, MI, 2011

Mrs. Kelly's JOURNEY HOME

I imagine my mother in heaven, still watching over us all and cheering me on. I never remember my mother discouraging me from trying anything. I still hear her voice saying, "You can do it!" When I was involved in community theater, she would proudly (and incorrectly) tell everyone that I got every part I auditioned for. We lived in a small village in Michigan near the town with the Purple Rose Theatre, founded by the actor Jeff Daniels. One day, my mom called me to her bedside and said, "You should call that Jeff Daniels and tell him you're available!" Always my champion.

I see her in heaven enjoying the company of her family and friends, and I hear her voice: *"I'm finally home and the tea here is heavenly! God bless."*

This poem, written by Henry Scott Holland, is often called the Irish Funeral Poem. We shared it at Mary Kelly's Memorial, and it inspired me to create **Mrs. Kelly's Journey Home.**

Death is Nothing at All
It does not count
I have only slipped away
Into the next room.

Everything remains as it was.
The old life we lived so fondly
Together is untouched, unchanged.

Whatever we were to each other,
That we are still.
Call me by my old familiar name,
Speak of me in the easy way which
You always used.

That it always was.
There is unbroken continuity.
Why should I be out of mind because
I am out of sight?

I am but waiting for you, for an interval,
Somewhere very near,
just around the corner.
All is well.
Nothing is hurt, nothing is lost.

One brief moment and all will
be as it was before.
How we shall laugh at the trouble of
Parting when we meet again.

Mrs. Kelly's JOURNEY HOME

At the Penn Theatre, Plymouth, MI 2023. Photo by Pete Mundt

The Play

After my mother died, I realized I had learned so much about caregiving and about what really matters. I began speaking to organizations, and I had the opportunity to tell a story at The Moth Storytelling Event in Ann Arbor. It was the *Tick-*

et to Heaven story. It was a hit and I knew I had something special to share. I began a professional speaking career, and my favorite thing to do is to tell stories. Brian Cox, a producer of storytelling events as well as a playwright and author, suggested I create a one-woman show. I thought about it for quite a while and then I decided to give it a go. I worked on the script for about four months and then met with Brian to see if I had something worth pursuing. He made many suggestions and helped me shape the story. Brian agreed to direct the play to bring it to life. After ten rewrites, we set up a staged reading with a group of friends and listened to their thoughts and impressions.

Covid was still a challenge, but we booked the Arthur Miller Theater at the University of Michigan for the World Premiere of *Mrs. Kelly's Journey Home*, presented by Pencilpoint Theatre, Brian's production company. A weekend of performances started it all, and here we are. Jim and I have traveled across the U.S. performing this very personal yet universal story about family. The most intimidating performance was in Ireland in front of an audience that included many of my relatives. Pro tip: Never attempt an

Irish accent in Ireland if you are an American. I was very worried about how my impression of my parents (with their accents) would go over in Ireland, and I was relieved to hear from so many, "You got it right!"

The broadcast of a recorded performance of *Mrs. Kelly's Journey Home* on Detroit PBS was truly a dream come true. Mary Kelly loved her PBS programs more than anything, and it is an honor to have her story shared with millions on this beloved platform.

When I was in the final stages of writing the script, I visited my Auntie Betty (my mother's sister), who is the last living sibling of either of my parents. I performed the entire show for this most important audience of one. I asked her what she thought and held my breath. She wiped a tear from her eyes and said with a smile, "Breeda, I don't know how you did it, but you got it just right!" There is no higher praise, and I couldn't ask for more.

Part 3
A CAREGIVER'S JOURNEY

I didn't know what I didn't know. All I knew was that I loved my mom. I had no training, and since all my elderly relatives lived in Ireland, I had no experience caring for an aging parent. We had the good fortune of a wonderful medical team that cared for my mother, but I had no idea what questions to ask and what to expect. Unlike caring for our children with Mommy and Me groups and a wonderful co-op preschool where we discussed our parenting challenges such as potty training, picky eaters, bedtime rituals, and countless others, when it came to figuring out the care my mother needed, I was on my own.

That's not actually true, but it was so overwhelming, it certainly felt like it. I was surrounded by a loving and supportive family at home: my husband Jim and our three teenagers. My brothers and their families provided an array of helpful and consistent support long-distance. While I was doing the day-to-day care, it was so good to know that they respected me and were in alignment with the decisions that we needed to make. Knowing that they trusted my decisions regarding our mother's care was a huge stress reducer. Not every family can say this, and I have learned that there is almost always one sibling who challenges the decisions made regarding the care of a loved one.

We were able to use our individual skills to divide up responsibilities. One brother (and sister-in-law) handled the finances and insurance; another took Mom into his home for weeks at a time to give us a break. They all called her frequently and came to visit when they were able. It wasn't perfect; there were conflicts and frustrations. Caring for an aging parent is never simple or smooth, but we did our best. That's the important thing to remember. On any given day, all we can do is our best. Some days are better than others.

Try to remember this the next time you get frustrated with someone you are caring for (and you will) and they get fixated on something (and they will). Just stop, take a deep breath, and step into their world.

I learned that caregiving isn't for sissies. It's a messy business and an isolating one at that. It's not for everyone. Our caregiving situation happened because we had the space, a big old farmhouse that featured a first-floor bedroom and full bathroom. If I have learned one thing it is this: Never underestimate the value of a first-floor bathroom. You can create a first-floor bedroom easily enough. A bathroom is another matter altogether. I realized that we are all temporarily abled. We are one misstep away from broken bones or knee surgery, and a two-story house can become a huge challenge without an accessible bathroom. Also, my work-from-home job allowed me the ability to be with my mother most of the time. Not everyone has that flexibility.

The biggest factor was my mother herself. She had always been an easy person, and with the exception of the delirium episodes, she was not difficult. She was also never violent. This is an important point to consider. While many families make promises regarding elder care, until you are in the thick of it, you don't know what the future will hold. Your sweet, mellow father who develops dementia could experience dramatic personality changes that make living together unsafe. Apart from your personal safety, the safety of your person needing care is a major consideration. Wandering and ingesting drugs/alcohol or unsafe foods are just some of the challenges. At this stage, safety is your guiding light when it comes to deciding where your person lives. If you made a promise never to place your person in a care facility (sidebar: please don't ever promise that) and now their care exceeds your capabilities or safety is the issue, you have to make the best decision on their behalf given the current situation.

One of the most important lessons I learned was how essential self-care is. I also learned how difficult it can be to find the time, energy, and resources to "take a break before you break." Giving yourself permission to take a break is a huge step in taking care of yourself. When I was a child, my mother used to take a break every day to watch her soap opera, *As the World Turns*. I can still hear the theme music and see that globe turning on the screen. She called it her "story." She made herself a cup of tea and sat down, put her feet up, and watched her program. Then she got up and went back to cooking, cleaning, and caring for five children.

Our lives are different. We are always on the go with to-do lists longer than Santa's. But it's not noble to be a rundown, exhausted, and cranky caregiver. You will feel better, be more effective, and be a happier person when you take care of yourself. Figure out what works for you and make sure you take time for yourself, every day. I learned so much that I wrote a book about it. Here are a few excerpts from ***The Caregiver Coffeebreak***:

Take a Break Before You Break

Lower your standards. It is not possible to have an immaculate house, a perfect wardrobe, a well-stocked pantry, well-adjusted children, a fascinating career, a great relationship, and be an effective caregiver. I honestly don't think it's possible to have three of those things at the same time.

We imagine that everybody else is doing life better than we are. We think other caregivers never lose their cool, prepare better meals, manage their household cheerfully, and are perfect parents, spouses, and daughters/sons. It's a lie. The truth is that we need to pick our priorities and do what needs to be done in that moment. Adjust your life to your circumstances. One day you will have the time and energy to clean the baseboards and paint the living room. Until then, don't feel guilty about all those things you could be doing. Take care of yourself.

Tea for One. Pour yourself a cuppa. Whether it's tea or coffee or even an adult beverage, find a cozy spot to enjoy a few minutes with a cup or a mug. My mother believed that a hot cup of tea cured just about everything. It's soothing and you just can't drink it fast. Take a moment and find that spot on the porch, in a comfy chair, in a bedroom, or if you have to, go in the basement. Create a little oasis for yourself and focus on enjoying that singular cup of comfort. An intentional short break can do more good than you can ever imagine.

Talk to Yourself. We believe what we tell ourselves. Self-talk is powerful and can be transformative. If you are constantly putting yourself down with phrases like, "I am such a bad daughter," "I'm so bad at taking care of Mom," or "I hate my life," it's even harder to do all the things you need to do as a caregiver. Be gentle with yourself and choose kind words. Catch yourself when you are feeling negative and flip it around. "I'm doing the best that I can. I am here." "I'm learning how to take care of Mom." "This is a really hard time in my life and I'm doing my best. It won't last forever." You can't control the circumstances, but you can control your reactions and how you talk to yourself.

Minimize Toxic Exposure. Toxic people can suck the life out of you. Whether they are clueless family members or unreliable friends who cause stress by not following through on promises to help, it can be toxic and detrimental to your health. Don't engage in the drama. That's why we have Netflix. You can find plenty of drama there and you can turn it off when you've had enough. Be polite but firm. Find ways to minimize your exposure to toxic people if you can't eliminate them from your life. At the very least, consider the source when they say something unkind. Don't give them the power to upset you. Boundaries are good and you are doing the best you can.

Guilt. Let It Go. It's not helpful and it can exhaust you quicker than changing bedding four times in a single day. If you are doing everything you can to take good care of your person and you feel guilty that you are not doing enough, you are wasting precious time and energy. You cannot cure Alzheimer's disease or other dementias. You can only do your best on any given day. Some days will be better than others. Cherish those days and remember what a good job you are doing. On the bad days, forgive yourself and know that tomorrow you will do better. Then, let it go.

Find Your People. Find an experience that has nothing to do with caregiving, something just for you. Your library might have a book club or a knitting group. Your church might assemble care packages, maybe a local bakery has a bread-baking class. I loved community theater while I cared for my mom. It was an eight-week commitment and there were weekly rehearsals with plenty of opportunities for volunteers to help out, even if they weren't interested in being on stage. I could go to rehearsal and immerse myself for three hours into another world with different people. It had nothing to do with my family; it was just for me. It was just fun and had an end date, the final performance. Some folks painted scenery, some worked with props and costumes, some helped sell tickets. I looked forward to my little escape and it helped to sustain me. Little did I realize that these experiences set the stage (literally) for the next stage of my life with my play, *Mrs. Kelly's Journey Home*.

Once a day. Once a week. Once a month. Create a simple list of activities that you enjoy and can look forward to. Some examples: a warm bath, a 15-minute walk, a cup of rich cocoa, a movie, a trip to the library, a drive to a local attraction, a visit to a nearby city, lunch at a favorite restaurant, treasure hunting at a thrift shop, an exercise class, a massage, or just reading a trashy novel for half an hour. Give yourself the gift of a pleasant experience. These can be planned and anticipated or spontaneous. Either way, doing so will help you be a better caregiver instead of a bitter caregiver.

Mental Bingo. Mind games are one of the best ways to deal with difficult people and situations. I play Mental Bingo daily. In my mind, I have a giant Bingo card. At the top are five categories (or more) filled with the words and behaviors that absolutely drive me crazy. I know that certain individuals will say certain things or behave in a certain way that will totally push my buttons. Instead of reacting in a negative way and giving them the power to annoy me, I turn it around. I anticipate and expect them to say or do the things that bug me. Then, when they come through instead of being annoyed, I say to myself, BINGO! I can't control them, especially those with dementia, but I can control how I respond to them. Try it and see if you feel empowered by a little mind game. Just don't tell the other person you are playing.

Fatigue. It's real and it's deadly. People don't often recognize sleep deprivation in themselves. Lack of sound sleep can produce impairments in your abilities equal to a blood alcohol level of .10—all the bad consequences without any of the fun. Sleep-deprived people experience changes in brain chemistry that make them crave higher-calorie food and reduce their ability to resist temptation. Don't let this happen to you. Take a nap, go to bed, and work on finding creative ways to rest. If you're exhausted because a loved one is in constant motion and never seems to sleep, make arrangements for someone to stay with them so you can sleep. It's not selfish; it's survival.

Farm it out. You can't do everything. Figure out what you are good at and what you enjoy doing. Enlist the help of family members or hire people who can help do the things that are at the bottom of your list. Many times, people offer to help and caregivers brush them away because it seems like more trouble to explain things and organize them than to just do it themselves. Or perhaps you feel that no one else could do things the way you do them and that won't work for you. Please let it go and allow others to help. Maybe it's paying the bills or picking up prescriptions or doing a regular shop at the market for the weekly items. Your place of worship or senior center might have volunteers looking for ways to help out. Allow them to help you.

Golden Resources

Here are some organizations that can provide information and help, often at no cost.

Area Agency on Aging. Your area has a dedicated agency designed to help you find resources and assistance from local resources. Contact the National Association of Area Agencies on Aging to find the nearest Agency on Aging serving you. Visit: **N4A.org**

Alzheimer's Association. This organization raises money to help fund research through a variety of activities all across the U.S. They also provide support groups, resources, and educational events for families impacted by Alzheimer's Disease and other dementias. Go to: **Alz.org**

Hospice Care. Hospice is an umbrella term, not a specific organization. There are for-profit and non-profit organizations. Hospice is often misunderstood and called in too late to really provide help. The goal of hospice is to provide comfort care rather than finding a cure. In many cases, Medicare covers the cost of hospice care.

Here are some links to get you started:

- National Hospice and Palliative Care Organization: **NHPO.org/find-hospice**
- National Association for Home Care and Hospice: **NAHC.org**
- Hospice Foundation of America: **HospiceFoundation.org**

AARP. Sure, you can get great discounts and the magazine now features rock stars on the cover, but AARP offers a treasure trove of resources for aging well, as well as resources for caregivers of older adults. Check out the basic menu selection and look for Prepare to Care section on their website for valuable information and downloads. Visit: **AARP.org/caregiving**

PACE. The National PACE Association serves communities across the U.S., providing services designed to keep seniors independent and living in their own homes. Services include Clinic and Day Health Centers, Medical Specialists, Transportation Services, Family/Caregiver Support Services, Rehab and Durable Goods, Medical Equipment, and Medicare and Medicaid Services. Services are limited to the participating counties/regions listed on the PACE website. Visit: **www.PACE4YOU.org.**

When you need help. There are many professionals who can help you sort out the dizzying array of options, forms, and laws that impact your responsibilities as a caregiver. While it might cost you a few hundred dollars for their advice and counsel, their expertise can potentially save you thousands of dollars and years of heartache.

- **Eldercare lawyers** specialize in laws impacting seniors: **LCPLFA.org**
- **Aging Life Care Managers** are specialized nurses/social workers who offer advice and help create care plans: **Aginglifecare.org**
- **Everything Mediation** might be needed: **Mediate.com**
- **National Elder Law Foundation**: **NELF.org**
- **State Health Information**: **SHIPHELP.ORG**
- **Veterans Benefits**: **Benefits.va.gov/personal/veteran-elder.asp**

Local community services like Meals on Wheels and Senior Housing Bureaus can be lifesavers. You may be able to find help from a member of a local senior group or a volunteer from your church who is looking for a little extra spending money by being a companion for your loved one, for a short time so you can take a break. The National Adult Day Services Association might be helpful as well: **NADSA.org**

On Hospice

Hospices are not all the same. I am a huge fan of hospice care and I truly believe it saved my life. However, as in just about everything, there are good ones and there are bad ones. It's important to understand what type of hospice you select, what to expect, and what your options are. First, there are two types: for-profit and not-for-profit. There are excellent for-profit hospices and awful not-for-profit hospice organizations. Generally speaking, my experience has been more positive with not-for-profit hospices. Currently, there has been a surge in for-profit hospice businesses, and many families have had unfortunate experiences with some of them.

Cautionary Note

Deciding on hospice care is a huge decision. The basics are that if a person is expected to die within six months, they are eligible for hospice care. This means that they will receive support and services to provide comfort, but won't be cured. That means no chemotherapy or surgery. Should a person have a broken bone, for example, they would receive care to relieve pain. This is an important consideration as hospice organizations receive a daily stipend from Medicare for the first six months of care. Doctors are able to extend hospice care beyond six months if they believe the patient is still likely to die within the next six months.

My mother was in hospice care for seven months. The problem is when unscrupulous hospice organizations enroll patients who are not terminally ill and expected to die within six months, just to receive payments from Medicare. Those patients are denied treatments that would extend their lives and potentially cure them. It is essential to work with ethical hospice organizations that are guided by what is in the best interest of the patient, not their balance sheet. You can find the rates of "live discharge" from hospice organizations at **Medicare.gov**. A small number of hospice patients do recover and go on to live for many years. However, hospice organizations that have high percentages of "live discharge" patients, (over 50%) are not enrolling the people who actually need hospice care. This is a red flag for fraud. Those organizations are taking advantage of the Medicare payments and the families who need support and care.

Caregiving can be a loving and rewarding experience. It can also be exhausting, overwhelming, and frustrating. The goal of caregiving is not to sacrifice your life for others, though at times it can feel that way. Taking the time to intentionally care for yourself is essential.

Self-care is not selfish; it's survival. I know the times I wasn't my best self was when I had just tried to do it all and I was totally wiped out. That never ends well. The person in your care will feel your stress and may feel guilty for being the cause of your exhaustion. Find ways to "Take a Break Before You Break." Everyone will be better for it.

**Mary and Tom Kelly.
A long journey home. Finally.**

ACKNOWLEDGMENTS

To all the family members and friends who helped care for Mary Kelly. Your love and support is greatly appreciated and will never be forgotten.

The Wilson family for welcoming the Kelly family and helping us to find our way.

Betty Biancucci for being a wonderful fact-checker and source of material. And the award for being an outstanding Godmother.

Brian Cox who made all this work possible. A great writer in his own right, his encouragement and advice made *Mrs. Kelly's Journey Home* happen. He collaborated on the script for the play, and his direction brought the pages to life. Now as an editor for this book, he keeps making these stories better and better. From the bottom of my heart, thank you, Brian.

Our team at **Arbor Hospice**, Linda, Beth, Cathy, and all the staff and volunteers who helped us on this journey.

Mrs. Kelly's JOURNEY HOME

Karen Musolf, M.D. Mary's primary care physician whose compassion and honesty stewarded us through years of challenges and whose kindness and competence allowed me to learn and become the best I could be for my dear mother.

Mrs. Kelly's JOURNEY HOME

The Play
Mrs. Kelly's Journey Home

"Breeda Kelly Miller brings to life a funny and often profound look at her mother's journey from her native Ireland through to the end of her life, charting the type of experiences felt by generations of immigrants and adults caring for their aging parents. This is a theatrical memoir filled with humor and poignant moments, with Breeda performing each role, introducing us to her parents, their families and friends. *Mrs. Kelly's Journey Home* will keep audiences riveted from the opening line to the closing blessing. It is a moving, joyous exploration of love, roots, and family." - Vicki Quade, Chicago playwright and producer

Bring *Mrs. Kelly's Journey Home* to your community. To book a performance or discuss opportunities, reach Breeda at Breeda@BreedaMiller.com

Connect with Breeda

And if you need an engaging keynote speaker for your next conference? Book Breeda at the links below:

Media Inquires: *Breeda@BreedaMiller.com*
Website: *BreedaMiller.com*
Email: *Breeda@Breedamiller.com*
Or snap the QR code below:

Social Media

Facebook.com/BreedaMiller
LinkedIn.com/in/BreedaMiller
Youtube.com/@BreedaMiller

www.ingramcontent.com/pod-product-compliance
Lightning Source LLC
Chambersburg PA
CBHW030139170426
43199CB00008B/128